THE BOY WHO TALKED TO DOGS

THE BOY WHO TALKED TO DOGS

A Memoir

MARTIN McKENNA

SKYHORSE PUBLISHING

Skyhorse Publishing books may be purchased in bulk at special discounts for sales promotion, corporate gifts, fund-raising, or educational purposes. Special editions can also be created to specifications. For details, contact the Special Sales Department, Skyhorse Publishing, 307 West 36th Street, 11th Floor, New York, NY 10018 or info@skyhorsepublishing.com.

Skyhorse® and Skyhorse Publishing® are registered trademarks of Skyhorse Publishing, Inc.®, a Delaware corporation.

Visit our website at www.skyhorsepublishing.com.

10 9 8 7 6 5 4 3 2 1

Library of Congress Cataloging-in-Publication Data is available on file.

Cover design by Erin Seaward-Hiatt
Cover photo credit: Sigrid McKenna

Print ISBN: 978-1-62914-433-7
Ebook ISBN: 978-1-62914-880-9

Printed in the United States

To
my wife, Lee, and our fantastic children,
Siggy, Casey, Fintan, and Marie.
To my amazing mammy, Sigrid, and to
all the amazing dogs I've known.
Keep the life lessons coming.
I'm ready.

CONTENTS

PROLOGUE

SOMETHING WAS COVERING MY FACE MAKING IT DIFFICULT for me to breathe.

I jerked up, clawing at my head like a wild thing. But instead of an angry farmer trying to smother me in my sleep as I had just dreamt, it was just a big clump of stupid hay that must've fallen across my face while I slept.

My name's Martin. At that moment, I was a thirteen-year-old Irish street kid who had been secretly sleeping in hay barns to escape the rain and cold for several months.

But at least I wasn't alone. Six dogs had adopted me when I first ran away from home, and they were now following me everywhere. We'd become a gang of strays and the best of friends.

"Dogs? Where're you all hiding?" My eyes glanced at the mounds of hay around me. *They must still be asleep*, I thought. They always tunneled down deep when it was this cold to make a nest for themselves. Icicles hung from the tin ceiling above.

The pearly grey light told me it was dawn, so I snuggled back down and pulled a thick layer of hay over myself to keep warm. My breath hung like mist in the air above my face. God, I was hungry.

I rubbed my mouth on my sleeve and caught a whiff of myself. Phew! After five months of living rough, I was definitely turning feral. No wonder farmers kept chasing me off with shot guns and blackthorn sticks. Who'd want something as wild as me hanging around their farm?

I wasn't much to look at. Skinny as a whippet. Grubby. Ears that stuck out like door knobs. Long nose on a long face. Bold, green eyes that didn't miss much. An insolent mouth that usually got me belted.

What instantly set me apart from other kids around Garryowen—besides the pack of dogs glued to my heels—was my shaggy tangle of mousy, brown hair. It looked a bit like a wild hedge, which wasn't surprising, given the fact that it hadn't been touched by soap, a brush, or scissors for months.

As for clothes, I was wearing a black duffel coat I'd "borrowed" from a backyard clothesline, the same dirty jeans I'd run away in, and a scruffy yellow woolen sweater I'd scrounged from a plastic bag at the local dump. Even more precious was a pair of boots liberated from a Garryowen doorstep. I'd only kicked them off last night because they pinched like a bitch.

I started reaching for them but froze when I heard a creak nearby.

Fuck!

It was Sean Moss, the psycho farmer who owned the barn. He was stepping off the ladder on to the loft. His big, hobnailed boots were sinking down into hay, and his huge, knuckled hands were swinging his weapon—a heavy blackthorn stick—around in lazy circles through the air, the razor-sharp spikes making it whistle horribly. His eyes were nailed to mine.

"You again," he growled. "Warned you, boy, what would happen if you came sniveling back round here."

There was no point trying to explain that the heavy rain had trapped us there that night. That I'd been so cold and wet, I'd risked sneaking in after midnight. There wasn't a person alive who could negotiate with Sean Moss when it came to protecting his precious territory.

Suddenly he charged at me, swinging his stick high. *Thwack!* Fortunately, he missed. "Where're those bloody mongrel dogs of yours?" he roared. "Know they're in here somewhere!"

The hay around me erupted as my dogs suddenly burst out. They rushed to stand in front of me in a line and their barking became frenzied.

Sean glared at us. "Good! Got you all trapped." He raised his stick and took a step closer. The dogs' barks were as loud as gunshots inside the barn.

Crouching in the hay, I stared at my dogs in shock. I'd known them for months, but had never seen them like this. Teeth bared, hackles straight up, they stood side by side facing Sean like the most loyal of body guards. If Sean wanted to hurt me, he'd have to get through them first.

They were magnificent. First in the lineup was *Blackie*, a massive beast of a Newfoundland, crouched ready to attack, with huge, snapping teeth. Beside him was *Mossy*, a liver-spotted Springer Spaniel. Next came *Red*, a tall red and white patched Foxhound, *Pa*, a plump, black Labrador, and *Missy*, a silky Skye Terrier. Finally, there was *Fergus*, a long-nosed wiry terrier. They were my closest friends in the world, and they were protecting me with their lives.

Sean Moss gripped his blackthorn stick tighter, loosened his shoulders, and waited. He knew we had to get past him to reach the ladder. "You freak of a kid!" he yelled above the barking. "Think you're so clever? Well, none of you are escaping my stick this time!"

Without warning, he swung fast and lunged.

Blackie tried to grab him by the leg but he was too slow. Sean clocked his massive skull with the heavy blackthorn stick, and the big dog tumbled backwards over the edge of the loft. I heard him hit the concrete barn floor below.

My heart skipped a beat. *The mad psycho's just killed my dog.* The stick whistled past my ear as I scrambled out of the way, just in time. He was going to kill me, too. I had to get all of us out of there, and fast.

Sean swung his stick at my head. I dived out of the way again. Each miss was making him angrier.

The dogs worked as a team, trying to get him to move him away from the ladder, but he was determined to keep us trapped.

"I'm sick of you and your bloody dogs treating this place like it's your own personal hotel!" he yelled, swinging at the dogs as they encircled his legs. "This time I'm killing the lot of you!"

There was only one way to escape. Straight over the side of the loft.

"Follow me! *Now!*" I yelled at the dogs and threw myself straight towards the edge, sliding beneath Sean's swinging stick and down a very steep hay stack. The dogs came tumbling after me, an avalanche of legs and fur.

Blackie was waiting at the bottom on wobbly legs, looking up at us hazily. Not dead, thank God. We crashed on top of him, scrambled to our feet, and bolted for the open barn door. "Keep going!" I yelled. Behind us, Sean was crashing his way down the ladder. At least he didn't have his shotgun. The dogs raced at my side across the farmyard. The ground was frozen solid beneath my bare feet, so icy it burned. *Fuck*, I'd left my boots behind! Once I'd jumped the low stonewall of the farmyard, I glanced over my shoulder to see the dogs sprinting to the gate to squeeze underneath. Together, we ran across the frozen field, the dogs fanning out on either side of me at a gallop. My feet were now completely numb. The dogs raced ahead, barking in relief.

"I'll shoot the lot of you next time I catch you trespassing! You hear me?" Sean shouted after us.

Yeah, yeah. You can't hurt us now, you stupid psycho. Sean Moss was only scary when he had us trapped inside a barn with a big spiked blackthorn stick in his hands. Outside in the open he just looked pathetic.

I raised a hand and waved it lazily in the air as I kept running. "Morning, Sean."

"Y'know what, freak? Your old man was right about you! You're nothing but fucking trouble! You're so broken, even your own father doesn't want you around!"

If Dad and I had a private war going on, it certainly wasn't any of this bastard's business. Pride skidded me to a stop and spun me around to face him. Insolence was a real old friend of mine, and I knew just how to shut him up. His weak spot was the same as any bully. All I had to do was make fun of him. Cupping a hand to my ear, I yelled, "What's that, Sean Moss? What are you jabbering about now, you old scrooge?"

"You heard me," he bellowed back sullenly. "Your father won't shut up about how useless you are. Wishes to hell you'd never been born, that he'd never clapped eyes on you."

I'd heard Dad say things like that so often, the words pretty much rolled off my back. "Yeah?" I yelled back. "Know what's even funnier? What everyone in Garryowen says about you. That you're the most miserable cheapskate in all of Ireland." There isn't an Irishman alive who wants to wear that insult. Sean's eyes bulged with rage. "Sean, is it true what they say?" I laughed. "That you count every piece of hay before you close your eyes at night? Wow, that's pretty stingy, huh?"

His face went bright red. "You shut your mouth, boy!"

The little devil of mischief poked at me again. I plucked a stalk of hay that was caught in my jeans and held it above my head, waving it in the air. "Oh no! Look at this Sean!" I called out, pretending to sound worried. "It's a precious piece of hay I've stolen from your stupid barn. Just think, now you won't get a chance to count it tonight."

His eyes were almost popping out of his head.

I was actually getting to him—and over a silly piece of hay. I wiggled the straw in front of my mouth and said, "Watch and weep, Sean. You'll never get it back now!" Then I shoved it in my mouth. I ate that stupid, wiry piece of hay like it was the finest gourmet meal.

His eyes were bulging so much, I thought his head would explode. What an idiot. Why didn't he just walk away and ignore me? I kept chewing happily, my eyes never leaving his. Finally, I rubbed my stomach as though deeply contented. "Mmmm. Thanks for all your wonderful hospitality, you bitter, old scrooge."

"You come back here," he blustered, "and my shotgun'll blow that insolent mouth right off your face!"

"Bye, Sean!" I laughed, my self-respect restored, and jumped the gate into the next field. "Okay, dogs, where are you? You can come out now." My whistle pierced through the dawn.

They burst through a gap in the hedge, paws flying, bits of ice spraying up behind them. They bumped around my legs, panting and grinning, relieved I was safe.

I reached down, brushed flecks of ice off their fur, and rubbed their ears affectionately. They looked up, tails wagging, tongues lolling, cheerful as ever. There was such trust in their eyes it was scary. No one could have a better gang of friends. "Guess we've just survived another night together, huh?" I grinned back and then started running. "Come on. I'm starving!"

CHAPTER 1

Two Dogs and Ten Humans

IRISH FAMILIES COULD GET VERY BIG IN THE 1970S, AND OURS was no exception. There were a lot of us in the Faul family—two dogs and ten humans, in fact. Back then, I went by the name of Martin Faul.

There was Sigrid, our mammy, Mick, our dad, Major and Rex, our two German Shepherds, and eight of us kids. We lived in a small semi-detached house on the Garryowen estate. Not in the pretty old village part, mind you, but in the new housing development nailed to the countryside next door. If you're ever looking for it, Garryowen lies just outside Limerick in the southwest of Ireland. To me it was the center of the universe.

We were such a big family, it was sometimes difficult squeezing all of us into our small house, especially on bad-weather days. Whenever it rained our poor house shrank a few sizes like a woolen sweater put accidentally through the washing machine. It also got much noisier.

Of us eight kids, four were girls and four were boys. And just to confuse things, three of us boys were identical triplets—John, Andrew, and me.

This might sound like a lot of kids, but the McManuses down the road had sixteen, and so did the Maloneys and the McNamaras. Some families even had more.

Major and Rex, our German Shepherds, were just as much part of the family as us kids. They were huge and shaggy, with massive bushy tails. Their enormous ears flicked around missing nothing, while their paws were nearly as big as bread plates. They looked more like wild wolves than pet dogs and it became their job to babysit us. Major and Rex went everywhere with us triplets during the day except to school. Even when we took them for a walk, we couldn't take them off their leashes once we left our yard. It was one of Dad's strictest rules.

"They're not bloody toys," he said. "So keep them on their leashes. The first one of you to let them run free will get his backside flogged raw." He grabbed me by the hair to check which triplet I was, looking for the telltale white patch on the back of my head. He pointed a grim finger between my eyes. "Especially *you.*"

Even though the dogs had been with us for years, the day they first arrived remained unforgettable. Dad had cycled his old, black bike home from work. He was a driving instructor in the army and worked at the nearby Sarsfield Barracks. Every now and then, he'd come home with a sack slung from his shoulder, full of left-over bread from the army mess kitchen. Usually he'd put the sack on the table for Mammy to unpack, but this time he lowered it gently to the floor, and then jerked his head at it. "Go on. Take a look."

John, Andrew, and I shoved our siblings out of the way to be first to the sack. But then the sack wriggled and we fell backwards. "What's that?" John yelped.

Dad leaned back in his chair and lit a cigarette. "Go on. Open the sack and get them out."

Mammy handed him a mug of tea and eyed the sack suspiciously. "Mick," she said in her thick German accent. "Vat is in that sack? It better be those loaves of bread you promised me."

2

We crept nearer, gingerly opened the sack, and peered in. Out staggered two fluffy German Shepherd puppies. They padded nervously across our kitchen floor, sniffing and gazing at us with big eyes. Their enormous ears kept flopping over and their huge paws kept tripping them up.

We stared in awe. "Aaaah! Puppies!"

Mammy forgot all about the bread. She dropped to her knees to run a gentle hand over their fluffy black backs.

We kids shoved each other, trying desperately to wriggle in closer.

"Don't squash the buggers," growled Dad. "And don't bloody pick them up either," he threatened. "I'll thrash the hands off the first little bastard who does. All their feet are to stay on the floor." He glared at us. "And if there's any fights over them, I'll tap them both on the head." That was his way of saying he'd kill them with a hammer. We knew he was joking—sort of. He raised his mug of tea to Mammy, who was grinning from ear to ear like a little girl. "There you go, Siggy," he told her. "They'll grow up nice and big to keep you safe. They're from the army kennels. Their names are Major and Rex."

Mammy's smile widened. "Thank you, Mick. They're *vonderful*." She bustled off happily to find something to feed them. And that was how Major and Rex became part of our family.

—◆—

Just like the dogs, we kids knew who ran the house—Mammy. To us, she was a princess. Her golden blonde hair was always beautifully styled; she had strong, perfect features, and was six feet tall. Her eyes were steady and blue. She walked through our cramped house like Nordic royalty.

She'd been born into a well-off German banking family from Frankfurt but her life changed forever when she became an exchange student at the London School of Economics. That was where she met my father while he was stationed with the UN army in London. The moment they met, they fell head over heels in love.

She was very strong-willed and wanted to marry Mick, this big, wild Irishman, and that was that. Their marriage was a strange international pact, a bit like Germany marrying Ireland, and both nations moving into a public housing unit in Garryowen. Fireworks followed—and plenty of tears as well.

Sometimes I caught Mammy looking out the kitchen window at nothing in particular. Was she thinking of Germany and Frankfurt? Was she imagining the wealthy life she'd walked away from? She'd glance over her shoulder at me when I came into the room, the dogs padding by my side, and look a little wistful. "My family had German Shepherds too," she'd say, fondling their ears. "Major and Rex remind me of home."

Dad was even taller than Mammy. Bigger too, not just in body, but in spirit. Whenever he entered a room, he filled it right up to the brim with his presence—and that was when he was sober. But when he was drunk and entered a room, you made damned sure you got out fast. Back then, it was considered a very manly thing in Ireland to drink a lot, and my father was considered exceptionally masculine.

Sober, he was one of the most charming men on the planet. However, when he was in the wrong mood he could win Olympic medals for drinking. "Another one for Ireland," he'd say, raising a glass full of whisky to his lips. He'd drain it to the last drop like milk.

Sometimes when he was drunk he was very funny to watch—from a safe distance. After spending most of his money down at the local pub, he'd zigzag his way homewards. This was quite a feat if you knew how many glasses of Guinness, whiskey, port, and brandy he'd had. Once he reached our doorstep, he'd pause to catch his breath. Swaying slowly, he'd concentrate on inserting his key in the front door. We could hear him from all over the house.

"Bloody hell, what's wrong with this lunatic key?" we'd hear him say loudly in frustration. The moment the key slid home, guilt usually hit him hard. How much money had he poured down his throat during the evening? How many rounds had he bought everyone? Was any of his paycheck left?

These questions were followed by the same amazing revelation at least three nights a week. He'd stand swaying at the door and raise his hands like Moses. "What this family needs is a bloody, bollocksy budget!" His voice would ring throughout the neighborhood like a prophet's. "I know how to save bloody money! This family's going to start learning how to turn all the bloody lights off!" He'd sway some more before shouting, "Do you hear me, family?"

Finally pushing the door open, he'd stagger inside and weave clumsily around the house in search of light switches. Major and Rex followed at a distance, watching him warily, upset by all his loud noise and manic energy. But Dad was oblivious to them.

He'd lean forward and flip off each switch like he was God switching off the world. If someone was in the room, he'd point at the culprit with a wavering finger. "What do you think this is?" he roared. "Shannon fucking Airport? There's enough lights turned on to land a bloody plane on the roof. Turn that light off before you bankrupt me!"

By then me and my brothers and sisters were smothering nervous giggles in our hands. We all knew when to keep our traps shut.

If Mammy was reading in bed, she'd just roll her eyes and switch her light back on once he'd left the room.

Job done, Dad would zigzag downstairs until he fell backwards like a collapsing mountain into his favorite armchair. There he'd drift into a deep drinker's sleep, head nodding down lower and lower, until it ended up on his chest like an exhausted baby's.

Show over for the night, all us kids would run quietly back to bed and one by one fall asleep. Except for me, that is. Upstairs in the bed I shared with my brothers, I lay very still, waiting for everyone else to fall asleep. My ten fingers would be twitching in anticipation, waiting impatiently for my father to start snoring.

Pesky fingers, they were, all of them natural-born thieves. They knew exactly where a treasure trove of coins was imprisoned—coins that were desperate to be liberated by me. Their place of incarceration was inside my father's trouser pockets. The ones he was wearing.

As soon as Dad's snores began to roll thunderously through the house, my fingers poked and pushed at me until I carefully slunk out of bed and crept down the stairs. They negotiated me around the two stairs that creaked and along the hall towards the living room. They totally ignored my heart which was thudding inside me like a trapped wild thing.

Think of all those lovely coins, they crooned.

In fact, my fingers didn't stop prodding me until I was standing right on the threshold of the living room. Terrified, I peered in. Dad was only illuminated by the hall light, but I could still see enough to give me second thoughts.

The size of him was terrifying, from the length of his legs, to his sledge-hammer fists hanging over the arms of his chair. While I was scrawny like a piece of skinned string, my father was six-foot-five in his bare feet and tightly packed with muscle from head to toe.

I swallowed nervously as my eyes travelled up the length of him to study that big head lolling around on his chest. At this point common sense usually kicked in. My brain would frantically urge my feet, *Turn around! Walk away now! Danger! Danger!*

Unfortunately, my fingers refused to listen. I stared fearfully at my father's face as each of my silent, careful footsteps brought me closer to his nearest trouser pocket. I was so terrified my heart climbed into my mouth. My ears stretched out even further on invisible stalks to catch any unusual sounds between each volcanic snore. My eyes stayed glued to his face, watching for the slightest clue he was about to wake up. I felt like a spring being wound tighter and tighter as I crept closer and closer.

What scared me most about my father was his nose. It was surely the ugliest, most broken nose in the world, so dented in the center that it looked like he'd been kicked right in the middle of his face. When I first read the fairy tale of Jack and the Beans talk, the drawing of the scary giant asleep in his chair reminded me of my dad.

However, even this fear couldn't turn back my delinquent fingers. They itched, wriggled, fidgeted, and squirmed until they positively *hurt* with longing for those coins hiding inside those pockets. I slowly reached out my hand towards his nearest trouser pocket and slid my fingers inside.

My father's breath caught mid-snore and his big, bent nose twitched as he started to stir. I froze, and sensing something behind me, I glanced over my shoulder.

Major and Rex were standing at the threshold staring at me intently. Their bushy tails were low, beating slowly side to side. I knew they were soon going to bounce over to me barking happily if I didn't work out a way to stop them. If Dad caught me, I was dead meat.

I glared hard at the dogs and angrily waved my free hand at them as if to say, *Piss off!*

They cocked their heads to one side.

Stupid dogs! I flicked my hand at them again and pulled the most blood-thirsty, cross-eyed ferocious face I could.

Mesmerized, they sat down at the threshold to watch.

Ah, to hell with them.

Desperately, my fingers took over. I leaned closer and let them slip all the way down, smooth as snakes. Down past his crumpled, damp handkerchief with its horrible sticky bits. Past his army truck keys trying not to let them rattle and click until . . . *Eureka!* My fingers finally touched treasure and tonight the takings were good. He hadn't drunk it all away.

I transferred the coins, one after another, to my own pocket. And before I could blink it was done. As I pushed past the surprised dogs on my way out, my feet barely touched the floor.

Fee fie fo fum, I just robbed a sleeping Irishman, I hummed. *Be he alive or be he dead, I've now got money for chocolate and a cigarette.*

I flew up the stairs and slid back into bed. Even though it was forbidden, I lifted the blanket and let Major and Rex crawl underneath. I rolled on my back next to Andrew, my heart still beating crazily.

First thing next morning, I was in Mr. McSweeney's corner shop as soon as it opened with Andrew and John. Feeling like a millionaire, I grandly dropped the coins on his counter. First we bought an impressive pile of chocolate bars.

"Let's have three...no, four cigarettes each," I said happily to Andrew and John. "Hell, why not make it *nine* cigarettes each?"

Mr. McSweeney carefully brought up the precious cigarettes from beneath the counter and pushed them stealthily across the counter at us. "You'll all be smoking sooner or later anyway," he grumbled as his fingers happily wrapped themselves around my coins.

Reluctantly, I watched the beautiful things slide across the counter to their new owner.

⟋⟍

There were other times, however, when my dad drank and he wasn't funny at all. We knew those evenings straightaway. They were the nights when the door slammed back on its hinges, shaking the whole house, and he marched inside yelling. I hardly knew what he was roaring about because I was too busy rolling myself into a ball beneath my blanket and jamming my hands against my ears as tightly as I could.

Those evenings turned into long nights in which screams flew around the house, followed by insults, curses, plates, glasses and furniture while we kids hid ourselves like mice.

Andrew, John, and I usually wriggled under our bed and lay with our arms around each other, rocking in unison. Sometimes we snuck downstairs, risking our lives to grab Major and Rex and drag them up to our bedroom by the collars so they wouldn't kill our father. Together, the five of us hid under the bed, shoulder to shoulder.

Now and again Major and Rex would growl deep in their throats when things got very loud or Mammy screamed. We'd tighten our hold on their collars and shush them. Huddling up closer to their bodies, we buried our faces in their thick, soft fur.

The raging storm only ended when the alcohol finally overwhelmed my father and he fell asleep. As soon as everything fell silent, Andrew, John, and I crept through the house, the dogs padding at our heels, and searched everywhere until we found Mammy. We hugged her tightly as we could while the dogs licked her hands, her legs, anywhere they could reach.

"Don't worry," we told her fiercely through our hugs. "Everything will be okay."

"Yes," she'd say over our heads. "Thank you. Of course, everything will be okay now."

The only good thing about those nights was the terrible price my father would have to pay the next day. Karma would come calling in the form of a thumping, great hangover. No other vengeance could have been crueler. Even I was impressed by how vicious they were. And sometimes when my dad woke up, I was the only member of the family around. Ha! Such fun.

First his body would twitch. Then his eyelids would crack open to the barest of slits. At the first ambush of sunlight, he'd groan deeply—a truly tortured sound. Finally, without moving his head, his eyes began to cautiously roam around the room in search of help. Carefully, he'd focus, trying to find someone— anyone—to help him. And there would be me.

"Martin?" he'd whisper, wetting his lips slowly like a man dying of thirst.

I knew what he wanted.

On really bad hangover mornings, my father would easily have swapped his soul for a mug of scalding hot tea. Especially if it had ten heaping spoonfuls of sugar in it. Tea and sugar was the hangover cure he swore by.

"Martin?" he'd whisper again mournfully.

"Yeah, what?" I'd ask, looking him over without much interest.

He usually looked sicker than a dead dog on these mornings, but I couldn't push the memory of his bullying roars and Mammy's screams out of my head. On one such morning I looked at him coldly and said nothing.

"For the love of God, Martin, a cup of tea for your old dad," he begged. He looked pitiful.

That little devil of mischief sitting somewhere on my shoulder poked at me. Yeah, I could think of something funny to pay him back for last night alright. I cocked my head, as though hearing something from outside the room. "Hold on. Is that someone calling me? Sorry, Dad, I'd better go."

His eyes widened. "No," he begged, desperate. "I'm dying. *A cup of tea*—that's all I'm asking for. Run and make one for me, son, *please.*"

My hyperactive feet could never stay still at the best of times but now they were almost doing a jig on the spot. They always came alive when they knew I'd have to run fast for my life. *La-la-la.* This was actually turning out to be quite fun. Major and Rex padded into the room. Even better.

"What are those bloody dogs doing inside?" whimpered my father, trying to sound angry.

I rubbed the dogs' big shoulders happily while they wagged their huge tails, grinning back at me. Time to put my little plan into action. "Hello, boys. How are you?" I asked cheerfully, raising my voice.

"Please," mumbled my father, shutting his eyes. "The noise. Oh my God, my head. I think it's going to fall off. Please, for the love of God, keep your voice down."

11

I cocked my head again as if my ears were trying to catch the slightest sound. "Can you hear Mammy calling, dogs? I'm sure I can. Yep, that's her." My voice was increasing in volume with each word I spoke.

My father guessed what I was about to do. His eyes flew open in horror. "No, please, no!" he begged.

But it was too late. Vengeance would be mine that morning. I swung around, hollering as forcefully as I could, "Coming straight away, Mammy! Be with you in a moment!"

Major and Rex did their part too, barking as noisily as they could.

My father's hands were clutching his head as if it were about to implode. His eyes were squeezing themselves inside out.

I flew for the door just as my dad shot out of his chair. His enraged bellows followed me down the passage as I bolted towards the front gate.

"You little bastard!" he roared. "I should have turned off your bloody incubator when you were a baby! Get back here this second!"

I kept running.

"Get back here and make me a cup of tea before I flog the living hide off you!"

Funny, I've always been fond of a nice cup of tea ever since.

―――

Of course, my father also had his good points or he wouldn't have had so many friends. Nor would Mammy have married him.

"No one can make me laugh like Mick," she used to say. One of the things Mammy loved most about my father was the way he teased the German seriousness out of her. He constantly had her in stitches. "Stop, Mick! Stop making me laugh so much. I have vork to do!"

Other times he could drive her crazy with his unexpected pranks, like the time he brought a tiny cassette recorder home.

Knowing she was going to be extremely angry with him about something—probably over spending the household money on alcohol as usual—he carefully hid the recorder in his pocket and switched it on once she started ranting.

For once, he didn't try to defend himself or make excuses. He just sat at the kitchen table, drinking his tea quietly and nodding apologetically every now and then. Mammy, of course, had no idea he was recording her.

On this particular morning she was so angry, she could have given Mount Vesuvius a run for its money. It often amazed us kids how her head managed to stay on when she blew her top. She ranted and raved, screeched and screamed, unaware Dad was catching every single word on the cassette recorder hidden in his pocket. This was one of her *really* impressive explosions so the dogs and us kids bolted outside, leaving Dad to face it on his own.

But the best was yet to come.

Whenever Mammy's fury boiled over, it could take hours for her to come back down again. The more righteous she felt, the longer it took her to calm down. In this cooling off period, she'd mutter curses under her breath for hours, bang pots and pans around as she cooked, sweep rooms like she was possessed. She'd even clean the oven, the bathroom, and the fridge, all the while breathing through her nose like a dragon.

We knew how to read her body language when she was like this. If her lips looked sewn together, then she was still in a semi-explosive state, so it was safer to keep clear.

On this particular day, she breathed like a dragon for a good while longer than usual, but by dinner time she was beginning to calm down. She even served up the meal without too much banging. She still had a slightly wild look in her eyes but it seemed likely there'd be tranquility by the time we took our first mouthful.

At last dinner was ready. She looked around at us. "Dinner time. Dogs outside. Children up to the table," she said quietly. "Please."

We could see she was still dangerous. The dogs bolted outside while we kids ran to our allotted chairs, sat down, meek as mice, elbows off table, backs straight, no fidgeting, mouths zipped shut.

Mammy's eyes ran suspiciously over each one of us in turn, then swiveled back to the stew she was serving up.

In walked Dad.

We couldn't believe it. Strolling languidly through the kitchen, he was whistling a tune pleasantly, as if he hadn't a care in the world.

Wide-eyed, we followed his progress as he seated himself and looked at us benignly. "This looks absolutely delicious, Siggy." He gave her one of his most charming smiles.

Our eyes darted back to Mammy.

Her spoon paused above the stew pot. She looked him over slowly, a suspicious glint in her eye. "Humph," she grunted. When she went back to dishing out the stew, her eyes looked slightly softer than before. She took a deep, soothing breath. The last of her anger was finally leaving her body. Indeed, she was almost smiling as she raised a forkful of stew to her lips and looked around at us all.

Suddenly out of nowhere, a banshee screech erupted. It was Mammy's voice at full volume ripping all tranquility to shreds: ". . . and let me tell you mister big man Mick, you big dummkopf, you drink all the family money while I'm working all those hard hours at the hotel. Yes, while I work extra shifts to get the good things for these children, you do not help me pay the bills. You are the laziest man ever put on this earth, and I am zick to death of it!"

Forks half way to our mouths, we froze. This was obviously one of Dad's pranks.

Mammy stared at him stunned, her fork frozen in front of her lips.

"You are an impossible man, Mick Faul!" the screeching continued. "Why I marry a dummkopf like you, I will never know! Back in Frankfurt I have so many rich, polite men who all are wanting to marry a beautiful, hardworking woman like me."

Our eyes swiveled to Dad, at the other end of the table. He was eating his stew as calmly as I'd ever seen him. Where the hell had he hidden the cassette recorder?

Our eyes flew back to Mammy.

She was speechless. Her mouth dropped open. Then she leapt to her feet. "How dare you do this shameful zing to me! Turn that machine off zis second!"

Now there were two Sigrids ranting at my father.

Outside, the two dogs started barking and scrabbling at the kitchen door.

And as for Mick? Well, picture a man in an expensive restaurant, listening to Vivaldi's "Four Seasons" while enjoying his meal. He was completely shameless.

That's when Mammy went a bit psycho. Her English always fell apart when she lost her temper, but now she was practically screaming gibberish. It certainly wasn't any sort of English or

German I'd heard before. She desperately hunted for the tape recorder all the while screaming at the top of her lungs. She slapped Dad around the head and chest in frustration and as he started laughing, we kids decided it would be a good idea to run for our lives.

———

Mammy on a good day was a calm, efficient whirlwind of activity. She believed in a clean house and flew around at full speed, sorting and washing clothes, dusting, vacuuming, and sweeping until my head spun just watching her.

She always put on music as she cleaned. She loved symphonies and opera but when she cleaned she liked to listen to marching music.

While everyone else in the family busily helped Mammy, I stuck as close as I dared to the record player, the one thing in the house I was absolutely forbidden to touch on pain of death. Entranced, I would become lost in the music. Even though I was also forbidden to touch her precious records, I'd take off the marching record and replace it with an symphony recording. As soon as the music started, I'd climb on a chair and start conducting with a wooden spoon.

Major and Rex would sit staring at me in bewilderment. *What the hell are you doing now, you crazy kid?*

Not only did Mammy do mountains of housework around our house, she also worked long hours at the Parkway Hotel, managing the restaurant. When she came home after the evening shift, she always brought spare food from the restaurant kitchen.

Well past midnight, we'd hear her little Volkswagen pull in and would jump out of bed and race for the kitchen like a herd of elephants. We'd explode through the kitchen door and there would be Mammy, setting out all the carefully wrapped parcels in silver foil on plates at the table. Major and Rex circled her legs, licking their lips, their eyes glued to hers.

In each foil parcel was a different type of food. There was cheese cake hidden inside one and Steak Diane in another. Pickled onions, Tiramisu, pasta, salmon, roast pork, baked potatoes, chicken and mushroom pie. You name it, it ended up on our kitchen table, wrapped in silver foil.

Mammy always brought home two special packets of meat scraps and bones for Major and Rex. These she'd place on the floor near the sink so they could scoff the lot down.

That done, Mammy would kick off her high heels, light a cigarette and watch contentedly as we devoured the food. My older sisters would take turns making her cups of tea.

"Thank you," she'd say gratefully as they handed her the steaming cup. "That is vonderful. Just what I need right now."

In moments like these that little devil of mischief would give me a prod. The easiest way to get my mother's attention, which was something I craved so desperately, was for me to cram as much food into my mouth in the most repulsive way I could. "Yuck," I'd tease her. "Whatever this stuff is, it's disgusting." I'd grab more food off the table and wave it over my sisters' hair.

"Stop it!" they'd squeal.

"Stop it!" Andrew and John hissed, punching me in the ribs, furious I was making Mammy angry. "Why do you always have to spoil things?"

Even Major and Rex looked at me in disapproval, knowing I was annoying their beloved mistress.

However, nothing could stop me now I had the stage to myself. I kept waving the food around like it revolted me. "Yep. This stuff is dis—gus—ting!"

Mammy was outraged. "Shush your mouse!" she said furiously. "Stop being so rude! Shush your mouse!"

Later in bed, Andrew and John punched me for annoying our poor, exhausted mammy. I rolled up in a ball and took their roughing up silently because I knew I deserved it. I didn't care. It was worth getting Mammy's attention for a few precious minutes, even if it was for all the wrong reasons. Mammy loved me, of course. *If only I didn't have to share her with so many other people*, I often thought.

"Why don't you just run away and leave the rest of us in peace?" Andrew hissed in the darkness at me.

"You spoil everything," whispered John angrily.

Chapter 2

Irish Weather

Andrew's words turned out to be prophetic. When I finally *did* run away from home a year later, it didn't take long before I hit my first big obstacle: *the bloody Irish weather.* Try living rough when it rains all the time. Two weeks after escaping out my bedroom window, I found myself walking along the railway track outside Garryowen. It was hard not to feel sorry for myself.

Drenched to the skin, teeth chattering with cold, I trudged through the worst kind of driving rain searching for dry firewood. All the stupid sticks I'd collected so far were dripping wet. Useless.

I shut my eyes. Why couldn't Ireland be sunny like Australia, the Caribbean, or California? I tried to summon the last scraps of my optimism. "Go on, Martin," I said grimly, spitting out rain. "Pretend you're walking along a tropical beach and it's so hot, you're just about to stretch out and sunbathe." A gust of wind battered against me as rain poured down harder. Nope—not even my optimistic imagination could work in this filthy weather.

In the two weeks since I'd run away I'd come to *hate* rain. It was a complete bastard of a thing to deal with. Since I couldn't stay dry for very long, my hands were becoming strangely white and wrinkled from constantly being wet. My feet were becoming large, clammy, over-sized white prunes. My woolen sweater was slowly melting into my skin like soggy pasta. It was impossible to stay dry, even if I'd any spare clothes to change into.

Since there was obviously no dry firewood to be found out here, I kept trudging along the railway track to my secret hideout. This was a concrete culvert running under the tracks like a mini tunnel. At last I came upon it, shoved the wet firewood under my arm, and carefully skidded down the embankment to the entrance. I glanced around, then ducked and crawled inside the arched tunnel.

The place looked just as gloomy and dismal as ever. The dampness leaked down the walls in streaks. Bits of concrete were crumbling off the ceiling. The ceiling was so low, I couldn't stand up. However, it was dry down here, thank God. One thing I'd started doing since I'd run away was talking aloud to myself. "Jesus, it's lonely living on my own."

I dumped the wet firewood in a corner and gripped my stomach as a ferocious pang of hunger ripped through me. Luckily, I knew where there was something hot to eat. It was just a matter of dodging past a suspicious mother of a farmer and sneaking inside her farmhouse kitchen.

Taking a deep breath, I moved off fast in the direction of Stevie Murphy's farm. It wasn't long before I was crawling through a gap in his hedge, then under his barbed wire fence and slogging across his field. One of his cows turned to stare at me, slowly munching a mouthful of grass.

"Easy for you," I said. "Wish I could eat grass too."

Stealing food was always the most dangerous thing I did. I was terrified of getting caught because the farmer would be sure to call the Gardaí. Soon I was hiding under a window of the Murphy farmhouse. I popped my head up to peek inside.

From my foraging raids around the district, I knew Stevie usually was out working at this hour before lunch while his mother, Mrs. Murphy, went shopping in Garryowen.

Yep. My eyes spied my target straight away. As usual, Mrs. Murphy had left a big pot of stew simmering on the stove. But was she still inside? That was the question.

Bugger it. I was too hungry to care. I'd do a fast raid in and out.

Chickens and ducks scattered in outrage as I ran for the kitchen door and pushed it open. The delicious aroma of Mrs. Murphy's stew hit me like a magic spell. I wobbled on my feet, nearly fainting. I grabbed a spoon, lifted the lid, and my nose sucked in the incredible smell as my spoon plunged into the rich gravy and lifted it to my lips. I vacuumed it up, swallowing in ecstasy.

So meaty, and full of potatoes and carrots. Rich with herbs and onions and leeks. Just enough salt. "Amah! Heaven!" I groaned out loud and took another spoonful. The warmth spread right down to my toes.

Mrs. Murphy was a divine cook—that's why I kept coming back to her kitchen. But I knew I'd better get out before she caught me. I found an old plastic container and quickly filled it halfway. I took one last lingering sniff before I closed the plastic lid. Then I spotted a loaf of homemade soda bread on the kitchen table, cut off a generous slice, and shoved it under my sweater to stay dry. Now I had a feast to bring back to my hide-out.

As I hurried out, I sent the chickens and ducks flying again. It was starting to rain once more, but I didn't care. Not with Mrs. Murphy's dinner to look forward to.

Back at the culvert, I swallowed half the stew straight down without pausing. I dunked the bread until it was drowning in gravy, then gobbled that up too. When I finally stopped to catch my breath, I glanced down to find some stew still left. Good. I was panting hard and feeling marvelous.

"Thanks again, Mrs. Murphy. That was grand," I said into the gloomy silence. "Worth ten stars at least. In a second I'll finish off the rest."

Then there was a low whine.

I looked up and blinked. *How weird.*

A Springer Spaniel sat in the tunnel of my hide-out. A little male, maybe five years old. Rich red-liver patches on white with a speckled chest and funny feathered feet.

"Who the hell are you?" I asked. I could do with the company but was in no mood to share my precious food. Especially not Mrs. Murphy's magical stew. I looked him over warily. He was a mess. Sopping wet, flecked with mud, bits of bramble twigs tangled in his coat. So skinny you could count every rib. His big, brown eyes fixed on me as he sniffed the air hopefully. His feathered, stumpy tail wagged uncertainly against the concrete floor.

I glared back and held the container close to my chest. "Bugger off. This is mine."

His tail wagged slower in despair.

I scowled back, guilt making me nastier than usual. "Go on. Clear off. Find your own food!"

His ears drooped and he started shivering.

My conscience prodded me. *Go on, you stingy bastard. You've got to give him something. Maybe he'll bugger off then.* "Fine then, have some," I snapped. "But then you can leave." I'd have to be made of stone to refuse him. I scooped some of the stew onto the concrete floor. One scoop, two scoops. I glared at him again, saw those pitiful ribs, and very reluctantly chucked down a third scoop.

He darted forward and started licking the stew up off the floor, his tail wagging madly, his long, floppy ears dragging on the floor. Within seconds he'd licked the concrete clean and looked up at me. If his eyes melted any more, they'd slide right off his blasted face.

"No fucking way," I growled.

Our eyes locked in a battle of wills. Pleading angelic spaniel versus monster-hearted, hungry boy.

I shook my head fiercely, drank the dregs as fast as I could, and banged the empty container down on the floor in irritation. *Jesus! Those eyes of his were like weapons of guilt.*

The dog went totally frantic. He dragged the container all over the concrete floor as he licked what was left, his ears spilling everywhere, falling over the sides. After a few minutes, I picked up the container and put it out of reach. "Okay, you're just licking off plastic now." I tapped the ground, and after some hesitation he padded nervously over. I let him sniff me and at last he let me touch him. I stroked his neck and shoulders and untangled some of the brambles. His ribs made me wince. "You must be living rough too. Are you an unwanted stray like me?"

He touched me with his nose gently and didn't move as I ran my hands again over his wet, silky back. He was like an otter, though a very skinny one. He clearly loved having his long, silky ears stroked. I laughed. "You *are* like me, aren't you? Just want a bit of affection."

He licked my hand.

Once again a dog was working its magic on me. When I got up to take a piss outside, he followed me. When I crawled back inside the tunnel, he was still glued to my side.

"What am I going to call you, boy?" I asked, stroking his long, soft ears. "You're sticking to me like glue, but I can't call you, 'Glue.' That's too ugly a name for a grand little fella like you." I thought for a moment. "What about Mossy? Because you stick to me like moss to a stone. Yeah. I like that. Mossy. What do you think of that?"

He licked my hand gently, thumping his little stumpy tail on the floor.

I nearly cracked my jaw yawning when the sleepiness swept through me in a powerful wave. It had been a big day. I propped my back against the concrete wall and wrapped my arms around my knees to keep warm. Something bumped against me and I looked down. Mossy was turning in a circle, curling himself up to lie in a tight ball against my leg. He settled down and gave a deep sigh.

I smiled. It felt wonderful having a dog at my side again. For the first time since I'd run away I didn't feel alone.

——◆——

Mossy's growling woke me. I was curled on my side and he was curled warmly against my stomach. His growls reverberated up through my belly.

I sat up, my heart racing. Who was it? A farmer? Some weirdo? The Gardaí? Shocked, I stared as a massive black snout poked its way through the tunnel. Two orange eyes glared at me. I caught a glimpse of the rest of its body. The thing looked like a grizzly bear!

Mossy jumped to his feet, barking in outrage. The snout disappeared. Heart pounding, I crawled after Mossy as he bounded down the short tunnel to the entrance. Side by side we stopped and peered outside. It wasn't a grizzly bear. It was a dog. A massive beast of a male dog. A Newfoundland, I guessed, which was pretty rare in Garryowen. He had an enormous head with dirty-orange eyes that stared at me unblinking as he pissed on a bush. The same one I always used, the cheeky bugger.

Mossy barked again and I looked around in shock. Two other dogs were wandering around the clearing too, sniffing everywhere around the entrance of my culvert. One was a wire-haired mongrel terrier. He was white and had a long pointy nose that was tufted with comically short, incredibly frizzy hair. He was mesmerizing to look at, especially the funny way he moved like a clockwork toy. He had dark, merry eyes with plenty of spirit and little V-shaped ears cocked high on his head with the tips folded down like origami. In fact, he looked game enough for anything. At that moment he was busily sniffing the ground, zigzagging everywhere.

The last dog was a big-boned black Labrador. He was waddling around, oblivious to everyone else, nose glued to the ground. He quickly found any scraps of rubbish I'd tossed outside since I'd moved in, even eating the paper.

Beside me, Mossy bristled. He couldn't believe these three unwanted invaders were wandering so casually around his new territory. "Woof!" he barked, outraged.

Before I could blink, the three strange dogs charged straight at him. I froze, certain they were about to rip him to shreds. Luckily Mossy went belly up and pissed himself in apology. I held my breath as they carefully sniffed him over. These three strange dogs fake-attacked him a few times to teach him who was boss, but each time he squealed loudly until they dropped their aggression. More relaxed, they took turns standing over him in a dominant pose, making him wait while they loomed over him. At last they glanced over their shoulder and bothered noticing me.

"Holy hell," I said in amazement. "What on earth am I going to do with you three rogues?"

First I had to name them. Since the black Labrador reminded me of a local kid I knew who never stopped looking for food, I gave him the boy's name: Pa. The massive Newfoundland's coat gleamed so jet black in the rain I named him Blackie. As for the white terrier mongrel, I'd always liked the name Fergus so that became his.

My little pack was growing: Mossy, Pa, Blackie, Fergus and me.

———

A few days later my brothers snuck up and surprised me dozing in my hide-out. John stuck his head in through one end of the tunnel while Andrew stuck his head in through the other. Perhaps they were trying to stop me from escaping. "Hey!" they called. "Martin!"

The dogs thought we were being attacked on all sides and went berserk. I launched myself at Blackie and just managed to grab him around the neck before he leapt up and tore Andrew's face off.

"Leave!" I screamed.

My brothers had their angry faces on. "Who do all these dogs belong to?" demanded John. "And when the hell are you coming home?"

"Mammy can't sleep at night worrying about you," added Andrew. "She was crying all through dinner last night. Come back home before you kill her with worry."

I glared back at them both stubbornly. "I'm not going back," I said. "I'm living in here until I'm old enough to leave and get a job overseas." Andrew and John stared at me as though I'd gone mad. *"What?"* John stepped up close to me, more angry than I'd ever seen him. "Enough, you've got to stop this. We promised Mammy this morning we'd bring you back, and that's what we're going to do even if we have to drag you home."

"No. I'm happier here than at home. I like living with these dogs." I rubbed Blackie's ears. "This is my new family."

Blackie growled low in his throat. He hated having his ears rubbed and even more, he hated it when I held him around the neck, but I couldn't let him go in case he ate both my brothers.

They looked at the dogs then around my gloomy chamber with distaste. "Don't be stupid," said John. "Of course, you can't stay here."

I let Blackie go and stood up to shove my brother hard. "Don't *ever* fucking call me stupid again." Then I turned to Andrew. "You either." It was the first time I'd ever stood up to my brothers face to face. They stared in shock. The dogs started growling uneasily.

I felt as if I were deliberately cutting the invisible cord connecting us, finally ending our bond as identical triplets. I no longer was the little brother they could effortlessly boss around.

Andrew, ever the peacemaker, tried to calm things down. "Shit, Martin, you can't live like this. You'll freeze to death when the weather turns cold."

I shrugged. "Don't worry about that. Just help Mammy understand I'm happier now and I'm safe."

An hour later, when they realized nothing was going to budge me, they left reluctantly. "You won't last long out here," said John. "You'll be home soon."

I watched them walk away together. *Yeah? We'll see about that.*

—◁▷—

A few days later the dogs and I were walking along the railway line when we spotted two more dogs. They were trotting up the middle of the track towards us. Both groups stopped to stare.

One dog was tall—a red and white patched Foxhound. He had a big noble head with a square muzzle and extremely long, muscled legs. He watched us carefully. Beside him was a much smaller terrier with tangled silky silver hair and a black patch like a saddle on her back. Her feet were tiny, her body long and elegant. A dainty fringe of hair flopped over her eyes in two waves while her ears were feathered with long, silky strands. Her graceful, feathered tail was tucked between her legs. She was clearly terrified. I guessed she was a Skye Terrier and wondered how anyone could have abandoned such a delicate little creature to the streets. No wonder she'd hooked up with something as big as the Foxhound for protection.

Blackie broke the silence, barking ferociously.

"No need for that," I said peacefully.

Instantly, the two strange dogs bolted down the embankment with my dogs galloping after them, barking their heads off like they wanted to tear them apart.

"Shit! Come back you idiots!" Terrified, I slipped and slithered down the embankment after them. I didn't want them hurting that poor little terrier. Thick brambles stopped me from going further. I stood helplessly on the edge, listening to my dogs crashing through the undergrowth. They must be chasing the two new dogs through the maze of tracks. The little terrier screamed.

Then there was horrific snarling and squealing. Blackie was clearly savaging her. *"Blackie!"* I screamed. That bully of a bastard was going to rip her to shreds and there wasn't a thing I could do because of these stupid brambles.

Then the little thing ran out into the open. Thank God, she was alive. My dogs came crashing out of the undergrowth and rushed at her. She bellied up, urinated in submission, and allowed herself to be sniffed all over.

Furious, I stalked over to them. "You bastards!" I growled, thumping each of my dogs on the back. They ignored me and kept sniffing the shivering little terrier. "You better not have hurt that other poor dog either," I warned Blackie, pointing a finger at him. Geez, I really hated him sometimes. He could be a real thug picking on dogs much smaller than himself.

There was a rustle in the brambles behind us and the Foxhound emerged. Stiff-legged, he walked into the open as though about to face a firing squad. My dogs bounded over but he stood his ground. There was a lot of sniffing and growling, even some fake attacks, then all the dogs shook themselves and relaxed.

I rolled my eyes, my heart thudding. "Bloody hell!" That had been close. What was it about dog fights that shredded my nerves? I guess it was because any fight among these street dogs could turn deadly within seconds, and there wasn't much I could do to stop anyone from being killed. I sat down and forced myself to relax, knowing the new dogs wouldn't come anywhere near me until my energy was nice and calm. My patience was rewarded when eventually the Foxhound and Skye Terrier walked across to sniff me over.

Up close they looked pretty skinny. It was hard to believe such beautiful dogs had been dumped and left to starve. Jesus, humans could be cruel.

"If you two want to join our gang you can," I said. "What am I going to call you both, huh?" I stroked the Foxhound's ears. "You can be Red. It's a good, sturdy name and it suits you, boy." He was a bit aloof but I understood that. I was a bit wary around new people too. "You'll come to trust me in time," I said.

Then I stroked the soft ears of the little Skye Terrier. She was much friendlier and stood between my knees, gazing up at me in gratitude.

Feeling jealous, Mossy growled at her.

"Yeah, yeah. Keep your tail on, grumpy head," I said unimpressed. I rubbed the little female's shoulders. "As for you, darling, you're such a dainty little miss, you can be called Missy."

I shook my head as I climbed back up the embankment onto the track. "Six dogs? I must be crazy." I was starting to feel like the Pied Piper. "Come on, you lot." I set off fast and peered back to see all the dogs trotting behind me, panting, and I couldn't help but grin.

CHAPTER 3

Always at the Bottom

WHILE I WANDERED THE COUNTRYSIDE WITH MY NEW companions, I would occasionally think about some of the things I missed at home and some of the things I didn't. Before I ran away, I have to admit our household was usually very chaotic. Yet at other times our house became the most romantic place in Garryowen.

Mammy loved to be spoiled by our father. Whenever he wasn't away with the army—and he wasn't drunk—he used to organize different nights of entertainment at our house.

Friday night, for instance, was Dancing Night. After the pub closed, Mammy and Dad would walk home, chatting and laughing, arm in arm. Upstairs in bed we kids would hear them and smile.

Next we'd hear the record player go on and sweet music would swirl up through the house. Andrew, John, and I would tiptoe down the stairs and kneel side by side, hiding behind the couch. The dogs would peek around us out of curiosity. All five of us watched wide-eyed as our parents danced slowly around the living room to Patsy Cline, Johnny Cash singing "Folsome Prison Blues," or Nat King Cole. All tender songs about love.

That's when we saw them at their happiest together. On Dancing Night it was like having a pair of glamorous movie stars gliding around our living room. Even I didn't dare interrupt them. Instead I sat as still as a mouse and watched in awe. When they were like this, it was as though they were surrounded by a special force-field, keeping them completely separate and safe from everything.

Saturday night, however, was noisier because it was Movie Night. My dad would pull the couch out in front of the TV, allotting each of us kids and even Major and Rex a spot on the rug. We could stay as long as we kept our mouths zipped shut. I'd lie between Major and Rex and take turns using each dog as a furry pillow.

We kids always had two shows to watch. One was the black-and-white movie on the TV screen, and the other was the much more interesting show taking place on the couch—the one starring my parents.

These were supposed to be romantic evenings for them, but I guess it was pretty hard to relax with eight kids and two massive German Shepherds sitting jammed around them like eagle-eyed chaperones.

Both Mammy and Dad had their favorite movie stars. Dad liked Gary Cooper, John Wayne, and Clint Eastwood. However, he had to keep his wits about him if Cary Grant or Gregory Peck appeared on the screen.

"Humph!" Mammy would snort, her eyes glued to the screen. Then after a moment she'd snort again. "Mick, why can't you behave more like Cary Grant or zat nice Gregory Peck? They have such vonderful manners."

"Aah," my dad would say, smoothing back his full head of hair so it rippled like waves on the sea. "But have they got my hair? Can you tell me that, Siggy? Have they got my magnificent head of hair?"

"Stop being so stupid," she'd say. "Manners are much more important than hair."

Dad would tickle her until she giggled against her will. "Ve have ways of making you laugh," he said. "And it doesn't involve manners."

"Vy I love you I don't know, Mick," she said, pushing him away.

My father would just smirk and say nothing, but he'd wriggle his eyebrows suggestively.

"Stop that, Mick. Not in front of the children," Mammy scolded him, slapping away his adventurous hand.

"Later then," we heard him whisper into her ear.

Mammy said nothing, but we could see her smiling at the TV screen.

Mammy was like my sisters. She loved to jump up and dance to the latest music, and she especially liked Elton John, who sometimes performed on the popular TV show *Top of the Pops*. Dad was horrified. He refused point blank to get up and dance to those kinds of songs with Mammy.

"Come on, Mick. Get your lazy bum off the couch. *Pleeze* come and help me do the 'Crocodile Rock.'"

"No way," he grumbled, patting Major. "Call me old fashioned but that fella wears high-heeled boots and skin-tight pants."

"Don't be such a boring bum," Mammy said, still dancing, her eyes glued to the screen. "Cary Grant would dance to Elton John," she said over her shoulder, after a while.

"No, he fucking wouldn't," muttered my father under his breath, but he didn't say it too loudly. Nobody—not even my father—dared to come between Mammy and her dancing.

My parents had a very unusual marriage, but there was no denying that they were crazy about each other.

When both our parents were at work, we eight kids were left alone in the house. I usually got into trouble for driving my brothers and sisters crazy.

When John, Andrew, and I were born, Mammy thought she was only having twins. When they wheeled her back to the ward, she started having contractions again. These pains got so bad the nurses finally realized she had another baby wriggling around inside her demanding to get out. So they hurriedly wheeled her back to the birthing room and I popped out.

When I heard that story, I felt like the unwanted intruder in our family. Even when I was with my triplet brothers, that thirty-minute difference between our births might as well have been thirty months.

No three brothers could have been closer than Andrew, John, and I, but, to be honest, this was the most competitive unit of our family.

"Having you three boys is like having a bloody litter of pups," Dad would grumble. "Always scrapping and fighting together. Now stop fighting or get outside!"

It was true. We were like pups. We argued over everything that had to be divided up between the three of us—the best side of the bed, the best shoes, the best clothes, the biggest portions of food on our plates, the most milk in our glasses, who got to be in charge of the dogs—*everything*. Being the runt, I constantly had to wrestle, shove, and push away my brothers just to get my fair share or I'd be left with nothing. Sometimes we even fought over imaginary things. Like when we'd lie in bed side by side, staring up at the ceiling, playing the Cake Game.

"Say someone handed us a big chocolate cake right now," John said one night. We'd instantly imagine one floating in the air above us. I'd even lick my lips.

"Of course, if we had that cake here *right now*, I'd have to get the biggest piece," boasted John, "because I'm the eldest."

"Well, I'd get the second biggest piece!" snapped Andrew. "Which would be much bigger than yours, Martin, because I'm the second eldest."

"Oh, yeah?" I shouted, sick to the back teeth of always being the runt. "Well, I'd go and *steal* that cake before you two even woke up, and that way I'd get the whole stupid lot!"

Andrew frowned. "You probably would too. Why can't you just make it easier on everyone and accept you always have to come *last* because you're the *youngest?* Then we wouldn't fight so much."

They both looked at me curiously. I was so angry, I could only glare back.

"John and I accept our places in the natural pecking order of things. Why can't you?" Andrew persisted.

"Because you wouldn't be so happy if you *always* had to be last like me!" I yelled at the top of my voice.

They stared at me in shock.

"No wonder I always end up stealing stuff! I'm sick of always being the least important person in this whole family!"

"Shush your mouses!" Mammy called out wearily from her bedroom. "No fighting. Have some manners while the rest of us are trying to sleep. I be telling you, please shush your mouses!"

"Or I'll come in and bloody shush them for you," growled Dad beside her.

Although we fought a lot, Andrew and John were definitely my best human friends in the world. They always kept a protective eye on me. John was the tough, strong one. I pretended he was like my mini-dad. Because he was a popular boy, he told the other kids in the neighborhood that if they wanted to play with *him*, then they had to play with me too. He also helped me play sports better.

Andrew was the worrier of our little family of triplets. I used to pretend he was like my mini-Mammy. He always made sure I remembered to brush my hair and teeth and wear a warm sweater. He spent hours trying to help me with my reading and writing.

As for me, I was like their naughty kid. They scolded me constantly for stealing and annoying Mammy. They nagged me to do my chores. Like all families, we triplets had a very rigid pecking order, and unfortunately I was *always* at the bottom. Another horrible thing about being an identical triplet is that I knew every second of the day what I looked like because I constantly had two more replicas of myself staring back at me.

I knew I had jug ears that stuck out, that I was puny-chested and skinny-legged and had arms like sticks. It was like having two brutally honest mirrors following me around all day. I also knew how I looked when I was confused, silly, or worst of all, frightened. Sometimes I'd stop looking at my brothers for hours at a time just to give my eyes a rest.

My father had his own way of telling us apart. "Which bloody one are you?" he'd say, grabbing whoever was closest by the hair. He was looking for the small, blond patch of hair on the back of my head that made me instantly recognizable.

Since I was usually guilty of committing some crime or another, "Which one of you is Martin?" was the constant question on everyone's lips. Unfortunately, my patch of hair gave me away every single time.

To the rest of the world, I was forever being lumped in with my brothers. Being an identical triplet can be the weirdest sort of hell. Sometimes it seemed like John, Andrew, and I were chained together in a cage with a flashing neon sign that read, Feel Free to Stare at Us Three Cloned Freaks!

Or try splitting a chocolate bar with two of your clones fighting over every inch. We learned the only way to ensure we all got a fair share was to hold each other's hair while we each took a bite. If anyone tried to cheat and grab more than his-share, the other two yanked the culprit's head back fast.

Sometimes our fights got so intense over the silliest things that we might find ourselves rolling around the living room carpet, punching each other over an extra slice of bread one of us had grabbed and half-swallowed before it could be tugged out again. It was enough to drive anyone crazy.

By far, the worst thing was the way everyone stared at us in public. I'd get paranoid walking with my brothers down the main street of Limerick, trailing after Mammy as she did the shopping. Even on the busiest days, there wasn't a person who didn't turn to stare at us open-mouthed as we passed.

I had my own way of blocking them out. The longer they stared, the more I retreated into myself. I'd block out all noise until it felt like I'd managed to pull the whole town down into an imaginary giant fishbowl. The sounds of O'Connor Street would turn eerily muffled, as though we were all underwater. Everyone seemed to gulp and stare at us like dumb goldfish. It was my way of dealing with all those staring eyes, but sometimes it didn't shut out their whispers, the worst of which came from women:

"There's that German woman, you know."

"Siggy, they say her name is. Imagine being landed with a name like that. Sounds like you're asking for a *cigarette* every time you call her."

"It's hardly surprising there're three clones of those kids, is it? I mean you do know about Hitler's *secret experiments* in the war, don't you?"

"Why doesn't she go back to Germany where she belongs and leave Ireland to the Irish?"

There was always a comment about me, usually because I scowled the most.

"I *certainly* don't like the look of that one on the end there. He looks like a nasty little bugger if you ask me."

I tried glaring back but their eyes were steely sharp, and there were too many to stare down.

Funnily enough, all the local businessmen in Limerick knew my mother from her job at the restaurant in the Parkway Hotel. Unlike the women, they treated her like a princess. Out would come the local accountant as Mammy passed by, dragging us along in her wake. He'd grasp her hand and kiss it while we watched on suspiciously.

"Good morning, Mrs. Faul." He pronounced our surname correctly—Fall, not Fowl.

Out would come the bank manager.

Same thing.

The butcher.

The doctor.

The real estate agent.

The big shop owners.

However, one look at the three of us, glaring like murderous little monsters by her side, was enough to stop them from chasing her too hard.

Not that it mattered. For Mammy, no other man existed on the planet except her beloved Mick. She adored him heart and soul.

—◡—

Thankfully, there was one place in Garryowen where my brothers and I weren't regarded as freaks—and that was on the hurling field.

What's hurling you ask?

Only the most wonderful game ever invented by the ancient Celts. Some say it's been played for four thousand years, while others claim it was played by the Celtic gods even before that.

My brothers and I came together on the field effortlessly. All our energy and skill rolled into a golden phenomenon that could make that leather slitter-ball do whatever we wanted it to do. We were the heroes of the local Gaelic Athletic Association in Garryowen, otherwise known as the GAA. Everyone yelled and cheered their heads off when we scored.

Of course, there were lots of magnificent, skilled players on our team. Some came from a long line of hurling families and each generation passed its skills and knowledge on to the next.

Each grand weekly match took place on the Gaelic Games playing field down next to the gypsy camp at Rhebogue in Garryowen. There were four adult selectors: Jack Sheehan, Paddy Quilligan, Brendan Reddan, and Viviane Cobb. It was their task to decide which position each team member played.

This triggered much smoking of cigarettes and heated words before a match. They took each game deadly serious.

"Better put Derec Power on right corner-forward because he's left-handed and it'll confuse the corner back player." That was Jack Sheehan, master-tactician and head coach.

Meanwhile, a different battle was going on amongst us boys. Before each game there was the usual wrestling over boots and who should have the least damaged hurley sticks. There were fifteen members on our team and not enough decent hurleys. We'd damaged most of them and St. Pat's had never been a wealthy club.

I always arrived late and would in variably be barefoot, having forgotten my socks or boots or both.

"That won't do. Won't let you on without boots," Jack said, trying not to panic. He'd look quickly around until his eyes fell on some poor kid.

"Yeah, you. Give yer boots over to Martin here. You know he's a better player than you. You can be a sub this week."

The kid turned pale. "But Mam bought me these boots brand new for me to play in . . ."

But Jack was ruthless. Winning meant everything. "Shut up. You're subbing this week." Seconds later, he'd swing back again. "And he'll need your socks as well. Good lad—that's the Celtic spirit."

A hurley is like a hockey stick, only with a bigger, flatter curved paddle. It's bound with metal strips that cut like hell when they hit you. However, in the hands of a gifted player, that hurley transforms from an ugly piece of wood into a thing of magic. It's a game of grace and beauty as the leather ball— what we call the slitter—goes flying around the field at high speeds.

Great hurling players are mesmerizing to watch. Their wrists flick and roll, graceful as swallows chasing insects. The ball is fast—heart-wrenchingly fast.

A usual Saints' game went like this. First, our selectors would parley in a corner, backs to us, smoking furiously, swearing and arguing under their breaths. They had to put every decision to a lightning-fast vote. Then Jack read out the team list to us boys and we either groaned or cheered.

"Derec Power, Roger O'Mahoney, Peter Muldoon, Eamonn Wallace, Tony Dawson, Tony Maloney, Shane Higgens, Pa Mullins, Jim McNamara, James Power, Seamus Downes, Peter Sheehan, Andrew Faul, John Murphy, Neil O'Brien, John O'Neil, John Faul, John Bailey, Martin Faul, and Rory O'Sullivan."

Then we crowded in for our big rousing pre-game speech from Jack.

"Now, young fellas! This is the needle match for the Under-Twelves you've all been hanging out for!"

We'd all scratch our heads—had we?

"But," Jack would say raising a finger at us, *"But* we're going to keep to the rules. Remember, you must all be honorable in battle and *always* do the right thing by the jersey." He talked about our green Saints jersey like it was the Irish flag. By this stage he was like Michael Collins, urging his troops into battle. "Now here's the plan. We're going to fight a hard, clean game. Got that? You're my Garryowen warriors and you're going to go out there on that field and do great battle against our enemies."

Then before we knew it, he was leaving Michael Collins behind and was launching into his most passionate and blood-thirsty speech yet, sounding more like a mighty Celtic chieftain. "We're going to fight that bloody bastard Claughaun team to the finish! Do you hear me? This is a matter of *life* or *death*! So get out there and slaughter those little Claughaun bastards!"

We'd yell our heads off in agreement, promising to slaughter our enemies. It's impossible not to get a little bit bloodthirsty at a hurling game. It's a team sport that really resembles a battle, where your hurley is your weapon and the slitter ball is like your enemy's severed head that has to go flying through your goals to score points.

The Saints had a few hard-core local supporters who turned up to cheer us on. Our favorite, Christy Flynn, always drove his battered old VW van up to the sideline and turned up his cassette player so he could blast Jimi Hendrix. "Up the Saints!" Christy roared out the window. "Kill those Claughaun bastards!"

The smokers among us eagerly bolted over to score a few cigarettes from him before the game.

"Disgraceful! That man's actually handing out cigarettes to those young boys." This was from a shocked Claughaun mother. "I'm going to make an official complaint."

"Oh, fuck off," drawled Andrew as he passed by, lighting up.

Seven or eight fathers arrived to support the Saints and began cheering for us noisily as the tension started to rise around the field. Somehow the selectors dragged us away from Christy's van, herding us out on to the field as the ref started blasting away on his whistle.

"Put those cigarettes out instantly!" he bellowed at us.

"Shit, keep your hair on, man," Christy griped, blowing smoke out his window.

Now the visiting Claughaun team marched onto the field. Unlike us, they wore beautifully laundered jerseys and shorts, their haircuts were neat and tidy, their socks were pulled up to regulation height, and their shoelaces were tied in double-knots as required. They stood politely in a well-ordered line. Their hurleys gleamed with polish and looked suspiciously brand new.

Moments later we much scruffier Saints wandered into position, staring intently at our opponents, poised for the whistle to blow.

Christy screamed from his van and turned up his music even louder so Jimi Hendrix could rage out at us like a deafening banshee.

The ref blasted the start of the game on his whistle, fired in the slitter ball and then, *smash*! The game of the ancient Celts began in a clashing of sticks.

The game flew by. There were screams of euphoria when we scored, groans when we missed the goalposts, and hisses and vicious curses for any dirty play. At half time we ran over to nick more cigarettes from Christy. Then the whistle blew again and the game thundered on until the last moment of play. We won! We reeled off the field trying not to collapse.

By now my heart was nearly bursting, my lungs heaving. I'd gotten whacked over every single inch of skin until everything hurt, but what else can you expect when you've had a heavy piece of ash wood bound with strips of metal bouncing off your head and body for an hour?

Now the best bit of the match—the after-party.

After the game, six of the heaviest drinkers on our team got to run down to the local pub, the infamous "A1 Bar." There'd always be someone inside willing to sneak us out a secret bottle of Bulmers Cider. It had a picture of a woodpecker on the label, and by God, it sure got you hammered.

For dessert we shared another pack of cigarettes that one of us had managed to pinch from some adult.

Smoking our heads off, swilling back cider, we re-played the best bits of the game. Yes, Sundays after the match were always great *craic*, which means great fun in Gaelic.

Later that night, Andrew, John, and I returned home, high from our victory, and climbed into bed exhausted. I lay beside them, bruised but at peace. We were loyal comrades, teammates and brothers. I was just drifting off to sleep happily when I heard heavy footsteps on our front porch.

Thud . . . thud . . . thud.

That would be Dad returning from the pub. I heard him banging open the door and walking menacingly up the stairs.

"Is that you, Mick?" Mammy asked sleepily.

As the storm broke and rage dinned their bedroom, Andrew, John, and I covered ourselves with our blankets. Eventually we ran downstairs and outside to the coal shed, covering our ears with our hands, pressing our faces into Major and Rex's shaggy coats. Anything to stop those horrible noises from upstairs.

The next morning, Mammy refused to say anything bad about Mick.

"But he shouldn't do that to you," said Andrew.

"This is my marriage and it's none of your business," she snapped. She thrust her hands into the sink and ferociously scrubbed a plate. We walked out, bewildered.

Later that day, Mammy received one of her favorite things in the post—a food parcel from her parents and sister in Germany. Wide-eyed, we watched as she unwrapped it. "Oh! Oh, look at that!" she said, clapping like a little girl. The parcel was full of treats from Germany. A packet of little, round ginger biscuits dusted in icing sugar, almond biscuits, rich lemon and lime jam, sauerkraut, tins of rich coffee, jars of Roll-mop fish, and black bread. Best of all: a tin of black cherries and a giant bar of dark German chocolate.

"I'll bake a special cake later when you're all in bed," she said happily. "Now I have some dark chocolate, I can make a lovely Black Forest Cake. It'll be a surprise when you wake up."

Of course, I couldn't wait that long. That night when my brothers and sisters were in bed asleep, I snuck down the stairs as quiet as a mouse and peeked my head around the corner into our kitchen. Sure enough, Mammy was whipping up batter for her cake in her big Pyrex bowl.

"Mammy?" I said softly from the doorway.

She looked up at me, then looked automatically for Andrew and John.

"They're asleep," I said. "Can I stay and watch?" I held my breath as I watched her tired blue eyes.

She hesitated, then smiled. "Very well." She held out the wooden spoon covered in rich chocolate mix. "You can start by licking this for me. I don't want to be giving myself a fat bum."

I felt like I'd died and gone to heaven. Unable to believe my luck, I quietly walked across the kitchen floor and took the spoon from her fingers.

She smiled at me. "Sit up there and watch," she nodded at a chair close by.

I perched on the chair and licked the spoon, watching her. She now had to melt the bar of chocolate, but first she cut me off a whole square and handed it to me. "Shh . . . don't be telling your brothers and sisters."

I put the piece of chocolate in my mouth and sucked at its nutty, dark flavor in ecstasy.

"Aha!" said Mammy. "Do you know what's missing?"

My heart sank. Maybe she didn't have all the ingredients and she'd have to finish making the cake tomorrow.

"This very good cake needs music," she declared.

My heart lifted again as she switched on the kitchen radio.

"Ah, vonderful," she said as the opera, *Madame Butterfly*, flooded out around us, filling the kitchen with beautiful music. She smiled at me and I smiled back. I watched as she finished the batter, then carefully poured it into the cake tin.

As she slid the cake into the oven, the most famous aria of *Madame Butterfly*—"Un bel di vedremo"—began its quiet opening bars. Mammy sat in her kitchen chair and kicked off her shoes. Surrendering herself to the music, she leaned back with a deep contented sigh. "She's singing, 'One beautiful day we will see,'" she said dreamily.

I let the music wash over me and watched the Black Forest Cake slowly rising in the oven with the smell of chocolate and black cherries wafting around us.

It was just me and Mammy together, her head laid back with her eyes closed, a cigarette between her fingers, looking every bit like a glamorous movie star relaxing between film takes, and both of us silently drinking in the sublime music.

I'd never felt closer to her.

Chapter 4

The Railway Culvert

IT WAS A WEEK AFTER I'D ADOPTED RED AND MISSY. THE seven of us had just climbed up the embankment from our hide-out under the railway track and we stood staring in shock.

A person was walking down the line towards us.

Who the hell was that? My heart began racing. It was a young male, swinging a nasty-looking blackthorn stick around in the air with intent. Bloody hell, was it someone come to beat me up? Maybe a farmer's son sent from nearby?

I froze. The dogs saw the boy's swinging stick and slunk down the embankment into the blackberry bushes to hide. I was just about to join them when I recognized the boy. *Roger the Dodger.* Another Garryowen outsider like me.

I knew him a bit from around Garryowen. He wasn't too bad. I relaxed and waited until he caught up with me, but I kept a wary eye on that stick of his.

He hadn't changed much since I'd last seen him. He was still short with flaming red hair the color of a fox and had big red freckles sprinkled over his face and watchful eyes that darted everywhere, noticing everything. He really *was* like a fox.

He'd earned his nickname for being so clever at surviving on the streets. Three years older than me, he was used to sleeping rough every now and again when things got bad at home. His father was extremely violent when he got drunk—even worse than mine.

My mouth started watering when I saw the cigarette he was smoking.

"Hey, Faullie," he said cheerfully, sauntering straight up to me. To show he meant no harm, he lowered his stick and handed me his precious cigarette to share. "I've seen you around here a bit lately," he said. "From a distance, that is. Where've you been staying?"

I took a heartfelt drag and handed it back. "Got a hide-out down here. Have a look." I led the way down the embankment and proudly showed him my hide-out under the track.

He crawled in after me then straight out again and shook his head. "What the hell are you doing sleeping in that rat-hole, you idiot?" He used his chin to point in a few directions. "Jesus, Faullie. There's plenty of comfy hay barns around here, so why freeze your bollocks off down in that dismal thing?"

I looked at him with respect. "Hay barns? You're kidding! They're always right next to farmhouses. Won't the farmers catch me?"

"Nah," he said airily. "You'll be fine. Done it millions of times before. Just sneak in after dark, then make damned sure you get out early before the roosters really start crowing."

There was a rustle of bushes. His sharp, foxy eyes widened in amazement as my dogs came creeping out. They padded over to sniff him. He laughed. "Jesus! What's all this, Faullie? Are you turning into bloody St. Francis of Assisi or something?"

I laughed. "Nah. They're just my friends. You know—strays."

Roger scratched his head. "Well, you can't be taking *them* around to any hay barns. Look at them all! They'll be impossible to hide. Stand out like a herd of elephants." He patted fat Pa whose tail was wagging hard. "First the farmers will have a heart attack to see them hanging around their precious cows. Then when they've caught their breath, they'll run and fetch their shotguns before you can blink. Shoot the lot of them."

"Yeah, I know, but they're my friends." I stroked each of their heads fondly. "I can't just dump them here. They'll starve to death or freeze without me."

Roger leaned over and tapped me on the chest. "First rule of survival, Faullie: Look after yourself first, second, third, and last—and all the other times in between. Believe me, nice guys come last."

He was only trying to help, but I secretly disagreed. Now that I knew these dogs, I preferred the attitude of the three musketeers. *One for all and all for one.* I looked around at the dogs. How could I possibly abandon them? They trusted me so much with their lives. I sat down and started rubbing their ears.

Roger the Dodger sat down beside me on the metal rail and handed me another cigarette. He even lit it for me. We smoked in silence. Cigarettes were like peace pipes for Garryowen boys. No one disturbed the moment when a precious cigarette was being enjoyed.

While we smoked, we stroked the dogs as they walked back and forth between us and laughed as they nudged us both greedily for pats.

I looked around at my gang. It was crazy, but I suddenly realized how much these six dogs were beginning to bring out the best in me. They were helping me become calmer, more caring, and affectionate. I was so much happier now! *Martin,* I thought, *do you know what? For the first time in a long time, you actually like yourself.*

I glanced across at Roger. Underneath all his tough talk, he was a gentle person. He was patting all the dogs affectionately. "No offense, but I wouldn't get too fond of them, Faullie," he warned me kindly. "D'you know farmers lay down poison baits to kill off stray dogs like these? Hide them in their hedges."

I felt my gut sink. "Yeah, I know that." It was one of the scary things I tried not to think about.

Roger looked at me curiously. "Anyway, why aren't your brothers with you? I don't think I've ever seen the three of you apart before. Had a fight or something?"

I squirmed and suddenly wished I was alone with my dogs again. They never asked me difficult questions. Or made me feel embarrassed or ashamed. Why did humans have to pry so much? "My brothers are still at home," I said, hunching my shoulders. I didn't want to talk about them; it made me too upset.

He shrugged. "Fair enough. Anyway, if I were you I'd think about moving into a hay barn soon. Cold weather's coming and you don't want to freeze to death." He patted me kindly on the shoulder. "I'm not trying to tell you your business, but I don't want to walk along here one day and find your body frozen like an ice-block down in that dismal little hole." He handed me a cigarette for good luck and disappeared up the embankment, whistling the latest Beatles tune.

I let out my breath once he left and patted the dogs for reassurance. It was so much easier not having humans around. "You lot think I'm great exactly as I am, don't you?" I asked.

They looked up at me, their tails wagging slowly.

"As long as you've got food in your bellies and we've got somewhere dry to sleep. You just want me to be calm and happy, huh?"

With these dogs I felt finally free to be myself. However, I was grateful for Roger telling me about the hay barns. They sounded well worth a look.

———

The first hay barn I decided to risk sleeping in belonged to Padraig O'Rourke. I had a good feeling about Padraig. I'd seen him around the area for a while now. He was an older Garryowen bachelor farmer and was quiet, well-mannered, and, best of all, a bit deaf.

I decided to go in at dusk, just before it got dark. Luckily he had no farm dogs. Crouching down, my own dogs tucked in tight against me, I peered through his hedge. There was Padraig's farmhouse, smoke curling up from his chimney, his radio turned up loud. Even from here, I could smell what he was having for dinner—sausages. The dogs started licking their lips and so did I.

"Keep your traps shut," I hissed. "Who knows if Padraig will come out with his shot gun if you lot start barking." I glared around at them. They seemed to understand the gravity of the situation. "Stick right behind me," I hissed, jerking a thumb behind me. I took a deep breath and snuck through a gap in the hedge, the dogs following quietly. We slipped through his farmyard like shadows. In a single file we crept alongside the wall, under his farmhouse window, and past his farm buildings until we came to his hay barn on the far side of the yard.

It was bigger than most.

Wanting a secret exit, I took us to the rear of the building and tugged at a loose sheet of tin from the back wall to lift it quietly so the dogs could hop inside, one after the other.

Before each hopped through, they glanced at me anxiously. They could tell we were treading on forbidden territory.

Once inside, I looked up at the loft. The hay was piled nearly two stories high, filling the huge space from wall to wall. "That's where we need to get—up there," I whispered. "On top of the hay." The dogs gazed upwards too. It was a natural hiding spot and they knew it. I looked for the best way up. The stack was too steep and slippery for me to climb, so I used the wall struts to haul myself awkwardly upwards. How the hell was I going to drag the dogs up here?

Not to worry—the dogs had worked out their own staircase system. They were leaping and jumping up the front slope of the stack, in a crazy hurry to get past me. It must be much easier having four legs and such a low center of gravity.

"Shush!" I hissed. "Don't you guys dare bark!"

They bounced past me grinning, then wriggled and heaved themselves over the edge onto the loft. They stood looking down at me in a line, tails wagging madly. *Ha-ha! We got up here first!* they seemed to be saying with their tongues lolling out.

I climbed higher until I could step easily on to the top of the stack. Beneath my feet, the hay was like a springy, thick carpet, surprisingly firm to walk on. "Wow!" I said looking around the unexpectedly large space. "It's like we've got our own secret cubby house up here!" After my dismal culvert under the railway line, this was like landing at the Ritz.

The dogs were wandering around sniffing everything in fascination. I walked over to a chink in the front wall and looked down at the muddy farmyard below. It was starting to rain again. "Yee-ha! Try getting me now, rain!" I walked to the back wall and pressed my face to peer through another gap.

"Excellent—the perfect look-out to see what's happening any-where around the farm," I murmured.

I turned to watch the dogs. The hay was making them so excited, like they were playing in snow. Mossy was running zigzag like a lunatic. Soon the rest joined in. Thankfully they weren't barking because in a big barn like this the noise would amplify like a bitch.

Grinning, I let myself topple straight back into a pile of deep hay. "Ah, thank you, Padraig. This'll do grand!"

The dogs ran at me, licking my hands, face, anywhere they could reach. I pushed them off with a laugh. "Looks like our gang has a new home, huh? Do you know what, dogs?" I said, sitting up and patting them all. "We might all be unwanted strays, but I feel like we *really* belong here."

Of course, they had no idea what I meant but grinned at me anyway. As always, if I was happy, they were happy.

As it got dark, we buried ourselves deep in the hay. The dogs tunneled into cozy sleeping burrows. I covered myself with a thick blanket of hay. "Good night," I called out softly. I felt myself smile as I drifted off to sleep.

⸻

A rooster nearby woke me with his crowing. He was probably outraged to find so many intruders in his territory. I opened one of my eyes a crack. It might be dawn but it was still dark. "Buzz off," I growled, snuggling down deeper into the hay. I knew we should be sneaking out before Padraig caught us but it was so warm and comfortable in the hay, I didn't want to move. I'd just had the most comfortable sleep of my life! The dogs thought otherwise. Hearing I was awake, Pa lumbered out of his sleeping burrow and waddled over to me.

"Creeping Jesus! Please go back to sleep," I begged him. "It's still dark outside." I buried my face in the hay as he prodded me with his wet nose in the back of the neck bossily.

"Bugger off," I said into the hay.

Pa, however, was soon joined by the other dogs. They stood in a circle around me, looking down in disapproval.

Oh God, I groaned. *Rise and shine. It's breakfast time.* "Okay, Okay," I grumbled to them. "Keep your hair on, I'm up." I patted them all good morning as I sleepily picked bits of hay out of their fur. "We'd better check if Padraig's awake before we start trooping through his farmyard," I said. "And for God's sake, don't any of you dare bark."

I dropped to my hands and knees and crawled to the edge of the hay loft. The dogs wriggled on their bellies to join me. High up here we had a clear view down through the open barn doors into the farmyard below.

Dawn was turning everything outside the softest pearl grey. Mist lay cloud-like across the fields. Padraig's tall black-and-white Friesian cows stood around in the yard below, every now and again lowing mournfully to be fed. Steam rose off their backs as though they were freshly baked, just out of the oven.

A door slammed shut.

"Wuff!" said Mossy softly beside me.

I put a finger on his snout in warning. He shut up and watched the yard below intently. We all did. Next we heard the metal crunch of Padraig's hobnailed boots coming down the concrete path. He came into sight—a short, fat man with a steady farmer's plod.

Fergus whined, and I leaned across Mossy to tap him smartly on the nose. "Shh. Don't give us away."

Whistling a lively diddley-dee tune, the old farmer hauled himself up on to his old Massey Ferguson tractor like it was a favorite old horse and brought it stuttering to life.

Good. If Padraig was busy feeding his cows, we could leave. "Okay," I said, "Let's move it, dogs."

Together we hurried towards the edge of the hay and sat down. From up here, it felt like we were on the top of a high waterfall of hay. It was a bit scary looking over. Taking a deep breath I pushed myself over the side and the dogs scrambled after me. "*Yeeeeeeeeehaaaaaaaaa!*" I shouted as I skimmed down the steep, tufty slope on my backside.

Missy zipped down much faster than she wanted to. Pa made a slow, regal descent, sitting very upright. Fergus desperately tried to use his long terrier nose as an extra brake. Laid-back Red slithered down, lounging back languidly on one elbow. Mossy treated the whole thing like a fast ride down a slippery dip. And Blackie, being his usual grumpy self, ignored everyone as he skidded down awkwardly on his rump.

We crashed into each other as we hit the floor, then crawled through our secret exit and scooted along the buildings until we reached the gap in the hedge. Once through we all started running in the low-lying mist that covered the open field. Mist always made for excellent camouflage.

It was time to steal breakfast. Reaching the railway line, the dogs and I started jog-trotting the three miles towards Castletroy. This was the estate where some of the wealthiest families of Limerick lived. It was also the place I planned to hunt for my breakfast.

At the railway bridge I stopped and turned to the dogs. "Wait here. You know the deal. We can't all go tramping through the suburbs in daylight or we'll stand out. People will start calling the Gardaí." I proceeded but turned again to find the dogs kept following me. "I said, wait *here*, you idiots!"

They lowered their heads and tails in disappointment and slunk into the brambles. Mossy gave me a long, miserable look over his shoulder as he slipped under a bare, twiggy bush.

"Thank you!" I snapped and kept on jogging. Every time I stepped onto the manicured lawns of Castletroy it felt like I was entering a different world. Cautiously, I jogged down the long, tree-lined streets past big houses with grand gardens and sleek, expensive cars parked out front.

With every step I felt wilder than ever—like a real tramp. I became aware of how my boots pinched because they were a size too small. That my clothes were dirty and tattered, and my hair was a wild tangle, with bits of hay in it. That hunger had driven my feet deeper into enemy territory.

My ears caught the low rumble of the bread van. *Right on time.* I ducked behind a parked car to watch it turn into the street and peeped over the hood of the car as it pulled in close by. The bread man hopped out, slid his back doors open with a bang, loaded his arms high with loaves, and set off down the driveway of one of the big houses.

He trotted up the stairs to the porch and carefully placed a freshly baked loaf of bread on the window sill. My mouth watered. Not long now. "Come on. Come on," I muttered, my eyes glued to him.

The van moved bit by bit down the street. With each stop, the delivery man ran up and down the driveway in a steady rhythm. At last his van rumbled around the corner and disappeared.

Finally, I had the street to myself. This was the dangerous part. I took a deep breath and got ready to dash down the driveway to grab my first loaf of bread when I heard . . .

"Good morning!"

Shit!

Heart thudding, I cautiously peered back over the car hood. A lady in a creamy silk dressing gown had just stepped outside the front door of the house I was about to raid.

Why the hell was she was talking to me? I wondered.

Turns out she wasn't. She was looking over her immaculately trimmed hedge at the man in a dressing gown on the porch next door. He was collecting his bread and milk, too.

"Good morning, Geraldine."

"Fine day, d'you think, Harry?"

"Marvelous," he said. "Ah, got to go. Toast and coffee beckons."

"Why don't you both stop jabbering and get inside?" I muttered grimly. My stomach was killing me with hunger.

My eyes swiveled desperately to the milk and bread on another porch. Sitting side by side, they were practically begging me to come and grab them. At last chatty Geraldine and Harry went inside.

I was ready to make my move when, like cuckoo clocks, all the front doors up and down the road opened one after another. There was a cheery chorus of "Good mornings!" and "*Ha-llo*theres!"

Fuck, fuck, fuck.

Now I'd have to dash around to another street if I wanted any breakfast. Running past more driveways, my stomach growled as I caught the beautiful smell of food cooking until I was almost drooling like a dog. Bacon, eggs, sausages, black pudding, tomatoes, baked beans, lamb chops.

On the next street, I spotted the bottles of milk and bread still on their porches.

Thanks be to Jesus!

There was no time to lose. I had to get in and out fast so I bolted straight to the porch of the first house, swiped the loaf of bread from the window sill, and kept running. Except I forgot the milk. Shit! I erupted through a gap in the hedge and ran to the neighbor's porch, grabbing their milk and bread.

I ran through another hedge, grabbed another loaf, then one bottle of milk and another. It was like I'd gone mad. I had more than enough for breakfast and dinner, but still I hesitated.

Just one more loaf, the little devil of mischief prodded me. *Think how good it'll taste for a snack later this afternoon.*

I was just picking up another loaf from a window sill when I heard the front door open behind me. I spun around to see a man with kind brown eyes wearing a silk dressing gown.

"Good morning," he said politely. "May I help you?"

I opened my mouth, but nothing came out.

He pointed at the loaf. "Er . . . we might need that for our breakfast."

We stared at each other a moment then he smiled kindly. "If you're hungry, you could come inside. I could make you some toast."

My eyes narrowed. What the hell was he up to? No one could be that nice to a thief stealing food right from under his nose.

The man held out his hands, trying to calm me like I was a wild animal.

I dropped the bread and bolted down to the corner to the bush where I had stashed the rest of the bottles and loaves, cramming them into my arms somehow. Then I didn't stop running until I reached the railway bridge—the edge of my home territory.

There I sank down on my haunches to catch my breath and glanced at my hands in disgust. They were trembling violently. Pathetic. "What's happening to you, Martin?" Even my voice sounded wobbly. "Why're you so terrified of some harmless, old, rich guy?" It seemed the longer I stayed away from home, the more scared I was becoming of people.

My stomach reminded me sharply that I still hadn't eaten anything so I drained a bottle of milk down without stopping for air and crammed chunk after chunk of bread into my mouth. I was so hungry, I wolfed down another loaf. That left me with only one loaf and two bottles of milk.

There was a rustle as the dogs barged out of the tangle of bare blackberry brambles, galloping towards me in excitement. My heart lifted at the sight of them. "Hello, dogs. Yeah, I survived getting breakfast—barely."

They crowded around me, sniffing at the precious loaf I held tightly to my chest. "Sorry, but this is for my dinner. You know the deal. I can't feed you lot until later."

They gazed at me mournfully. "Don't look at me like that. You know we have to wait until Brendan leaves," I snapped. Guilt always made me curt. "Come on, we'd better get out of this rain."

They followed me along the railway line to my hide-out under the track. Until I learned Padraig's routine, I didn't want to hang around his barn too much in the daytime. The dogs looked gloomily at the tunnel entrance, unable to understand why we didn't go back to the barn.

Blackie, grumpier than ever, nipped Fergus to show his displeasure.

"Geez, you can be a real sour puss," I said to him in disgust.

One after another we crawled down the tunnel and crammed together inside.

A grey, depressing drizzle settled in for the day. The dogs shook droplets of water everywhere while I lit a tiny fire with a few lumps of coals I'd kept stashed. It was a bit of luxurious warmth on a gloomy day.

The dogs shoved and pushed around the cramped space restlessly, snapping at each other. They were always like this when they got really hungry.

"Sorry," I said, shrugging. "You know the score—no dog food until after Brendan leaves."

One of the main reasons these six dogs followed me everywhere was because I stole food for them. At twilight every evening, I'd sneak into Brendan Mullins's slaughter house—the ultimate restaurant for stray dogs—and steal meat scraps and bones to throw over the fence to them. Trouble was, I couldn't risk going near the slaughterhouse until almost dark in case Brendan caught me.

Suddenly Pa's fat tail accidentally brushed against Blackie's front paws, and I had to pull them apart quickly.

"Whoa, now. C'mon, we're all friends, aren't we?"

Poor dogs—they were completely fed up. They all lay down with noisy sighs, their chins on their paws, and their heads turned away from me.

Suddenly I had an idea. "I know how we can cheer ourselves up. Tonight we'll have dinner together in the barn—like a real family. It'll be great." I could just picture the scene. All of us in the barn sitting in a circle, sharing a meal together. "Why not? We've never done that before." While I had my bread and milk, the dogs could have their meat scraps, and one bone each for dessert. "Look at us. We've got the perfect chance to be a really cool gang. Hey! What are we going to call ourselves?"

None of them were listening, but I didn't care. I laughed as a name came to me. "We'll be the Dirty Dog Gang!"

The dogs twitched their ears in irritation as if trying to flick away my bothersome voice. I decided to lean back against the wall and have a nap.

It'll be like we're in a Hollywood movie, I thought sleepily, huddling deeper into my jacket. *We'll be the Dirty Dog Gang.*

———

A fat paw rudely woke me. Pa was panting straight in my face. "Jesus, Pa!" I said disgusted. "Your breath stinks!"

All the dogs started shoving their noses impatiently in my face until I pushed them away. "Okay, okay," I grumbled. "I'm getting up. Keep your tails on."

The look in their eyes was unmistakable—they were starving. I checked that the loaf was still tucked safely under my sweater, then crawled outside. It was starting to rain and the afternoon light was fading fast. "I'm going to get soaked getting your dinner, dogs. Hope you appreciate this." It was always a big deal going out in the rain because it was so hard drying wet clothes and I didn't have spares.

We were on our way to Brendan Mullins' slaughterhouse on the edge of Garryowen. As I got wetter and more irritable, the dogs got more excited. Soon, they were bouncing beside me happily. When we reached the field bordering Brendan's place, I peered around the hedgerow for a good look.

It seemed deserted. Together we snuck across the open field and peered through the six-foot-high chain-mail fence. Then the stink hit us like an invisible wall. Phew! Brendan's was like a scene from hell. It was where all the dead horses, cows, donkeys, dogs, and cats of Garryowen were brought to be disposed and recycled into other things—hides for the tannery, meat for Greyhound trainers, and animal scraps for factories manufacturing soap, make-up and glue.

The dogs were avidly gazing inside at all the meat and bone scraps like kids outside the best ice cream shop in the world.

This was not a place for the faint-hearted. I started climbing over the six-foot barbed wire fence like a monkey. The dogs waited outside in line, their tails wagging furiously. Fergus yipped excitedly. "Yeah, yeah," I grumbled. "I'm hurrying."

I moved through the main yard where most of the bins of chopped-up animal parts were kept. Brendan didn't give a damn about health and safety rules. As I passed by the locked gates of the shed, savage barking suddenly came from inside. "Hi-ya, Buddy!" I called out. "Don't worry, it's only me."

Buddy was Brendan's guard dog but we'd become good friends.

I strode by the shed quickly, trying to ignore the sound of him pacing back and forth on the concrete floor. "Sorry, boy!" I hated how he had to stay locked up at night on his own, but I didn't dare rescue him.

I headed for the big bins at the back where the really meaty scraps were kept. Cow legs, bones, horns, hooves, and skulls. I barely noticed the gruesomeness anymore, but honestly, this place would traumatize a vegetarian for life. There were three big drums brimming over with meaty scraps—the perfect dinner for six starving dogs. I grabbed a sack and knife and started carving scraps of meat from the larger bones.

When the sack was full, I tied it closed with a rope and started hauling it towards the fence. "Bye, Buddy! See you tomorrow night."

As soon as I appeared, my own dogs leapt up and down, barking frantically. The noise increased as they watched the bulging sack dragging behind me. I maneuvered the heavy sack of scraps over the wire fence, let it drop to the ground, and jumped down. The dogs danced around me, whining and begging. I really wanted them to eat dinner with me in the barn tonight.

"Come on, you can wait a bit longer, can't you? It'll be our first meal together as a gang," I said to encourage them.

They just stared at the sack and drooled. When I didn't open it, they began whining one after another.

Geez. I didn't ask for much, but tonight I wanted this dinner to be special. Their eyes were still super-glued to the sack. "Okay, you can have a small snack now, but no more until dinner," I grumbled as I tossed a chunk of meat to each dog and firmly retied the sack.

They stared at me in shock. I knew they were really hungry but for once they weren't going to wriggle out of doing something I wanted. I started dragging the heavy sack behind me, heading for the railway track. Baffled, the dogs hurried after me.

The trip back to Padraig's barn was a nightmare. My back was on fire, my fingers felt like they were about to drop off, and I had a thumping headache from listening to Pa piteously whine the entire way home. The sack felt like it was stuffed full of entire dead cows, not scraps. All I could do was grit my teeth and keep dragging. Our gang dinner was going as planned tonight even if it killed me.

I somehow managed to haul the sack up the ladder and with sweat running down my face, I lit some candles and propped them along a ledge. Poor Padraig would have had a heart attack if he'd seen them but damn if I was sitting in the dark to eat.

The dogs blinked as their eyes adjusted to the candlelight.

"Right," I panted. "*Now* we can eat." I crouched down to untie the sack. "Hey, isn't this great? Aren't we the best gang?" I gazed at them happily.

The dogs inched closer, like psycho killers moving in on the prey.

"Wait, I want to put it in a circle." I walked around quickly dropping chunks of meat in piles on the hay, expecting the dogs to take their appropriate places. "Right-eo, here we go," I said happily. "Enjoy your dinner everyone."

Instead the dogs flew straight at each other and the noises they made were horrifying.

"Whoa!" I yelled in shock. All I could see was a mass of screaming, barking, growling, snarling, snapping dogs viciously attacking each other.

Bloody hell! They were going to rip each other to shreds!

I shoved my way into the middle of the fray to haul the dogs off each other. But as soon as I pulled one dog off, it quickly latched on to someone else. In between attacking each other, they frantically gobbled down any scraps of meat they could grab from the hay or out of each other's mouths. It was worse than Andrew, John, and me fighting over food.

Blackie emerged from the scrum, dragging the food sack in his mouth. Pa, greedy as ever, chased after him in outrage.

"Okay, everyone calm down!" I shouted above the noise. "That's enough! we're all friends here."

As I passed Missy, she whipped around to strike out at my ankle like a vicious cobra, her bared teeth like a mouthful of sharp needles. That was it. I no longer cared whether Padraig heard me or not.

"How dare you idiots mess up my nice dinner!" I roared at the top of my voice.

I tore them apart roughly until, still growling, they retired to the walls of the barn panting heavily. They looked like sulky pub fighters separated after a brawl.

"All of you, stay where you are!" I snapped as I sunk down in the hay to catch my breath. Then I remembered my loaf of bread.

Fuck.

When I frantically patted the front of my sweater, I realized my precious dinner was gone! I whirled round to see Pa with it in his mouth, ready to wolf it down in one swallow. I threw myself across the hay at him and yanked the loaf from his mouth.

Pa fled.

The loaf was a soggy mess, covered in raw meat and blood. Even I couldn't eat *that* gruesome-smelling thing. The milk bottle I'd carried around all day in my pocket was lying on its side with most of the milk gone.

Mossy was sitting some distance away, staring at me with his big melting spaniel eyes. As always, he knew how to play me like a violin.

"Hello, fella. This wasn't your fault. Come here," I said, tearing a scrap of bread for him.

There was a low-pitched growl from Blackie.

Ha! As if I'm giving you anything when you started the whole fight, you bastard.

Blackie didn't agree. His growl turned into a roar and he launched straight at me, knocking me across the hay in a confusion of fur and teeth. It was like having a grizzly bear over me with his huge teeth snapping inches away from my face. His breath stank of rotten meat.

Jesus, I'm about to die.

I turned my head to see Blackie walking stiffly off to a far corner with my loaf between his jaws. The other dogs watched in silence as he lay down and began ripping the bread apart, using his colossal paws to hold it in place.

I sat up. My heart was hammering away like it was trying to find a way out from between my ribs. I watched in a daze as that bloody dog calmly ate my dinner. *How dare he!* I marched straight over to him and booted him hard right in the gut. "You ungrateful bastard after all I've done for you!" This was the first time I'd really hurt one of my dogs, but I was starving, I was angry, and I couldn't think straight.

He bared his teeth at me, but I stared him straight in the eyes and leaned in close. "Yeah? You want to make this interesting, dog?" I wasn't scared of him anymore. He was just another bully pushing me around.

He leapt at me but this time I was ready and kicked him hard in the throat. He grunted, dropped back down, and glared at me.

I stared him down until he glanced away and shook himself from head to toe. That's when I knew I'd won. All of a sudden, he dropped his head down low and slunk over the edge of the hay and disappeared. I sank down, trembling.

For the first time I asked myself how safe it was living with these stray dogs—especially a creature as dangerous as Blackie. He was big enough to kill me and obviously not very stable either.

The other dogs were shivering and shaking in fear. I patted the hay beside me. "It's okay. You can come back now." They turned away, their eyes unable to meet mine.

I whistled softly, but they kept turning their heads away. I was hurt—I mean *really* hurt. What had I done now?

I crawled across the hay towards Mossy as I considered him my best friend out of the pack. He sat there keeping his head turned purposefully away when I moved closer.

66

"Hey? What is it with all this crazy head turning stuff, boy?"

Before I could touch him, he flinched. "I'm not going to hurt you," I said. I held out my palm gently. He backed off, this time yawning noisily as he turned his head away.

I was confused. The dogs were all doing exactly the same thing—turning their heads and slowly yawning, like there was a game going on but no one had explained the rules to me. Sick of feeling left out, I sat down and mimicked them. I turned *my* head and yawned in an even *sleepier* way. If the dogs were going crazy then I might as well join them.

The dogs went very still. They looked at me carefully and waited. I felt the hairs rising on the back of my neck. The second time I yawned, the dogs all lay down in the hay, one by one. It was like I was casting a spell over them. Intrigued, I yawned again to see what would happen. As though they'd just taken a sleeping pill, the dogs lay their chins on the hay and closed their eyes. The barn suddenly felt like the most tranquil place. *What the hell was happening?*

It was those two simple signals. *Turn your head away. Yawn sleepily.*

I crawled over to Mossy again and started stroking his neck. His eyes flew open anxiously, but when I gave another sleepy yawn, he sighed deeply and shut his eyes. After another yawn from me, he rolled on his side and dozed off. I glanced around at the other dogs. They were already asleep, and Pa was snoring gently.

I'm not sure, but I think we all just talked to each other in dog language, I thought. *Maybe when they turn their heads away, they're saying, "Please leave me alone." And when they yawn they're saying, "Just relax and chill out."*

I didn't know if I was right, but there was still one dog I could test my ideas on when he returned.

Blackie.

~

Around midnight, his massive shape appeared, casting long shadows across the barn wall as he slowly climbed over the edge of the hay. Half-dozing, I sat up.

Bloody Blackie.

Had he returned to attack me again? He slunk closer then stopped, sniffed the air in my direction, and growled low.

I was going to try talking to him in his own language. So I turned my head away and yawned in the sleepiest way possible.

Blackie stared at me in surprise, then sat down at my side. I was stunned! I'd never seen him so calm. I gave the two signals again. With an enormous sigh, he rolled over and relaxed completely.

He'd always snapped at me whenever I tried to touch him while he was lying down, but maybe now was the time to change that. I reached out a trembling hand and held my breath as I gently stroked his massive, shaggy neck. He was so unbelievably relaxed beneath my hand. I felt my skin tingle while a powerful energy flowed between us as we made our first true connection. He snuggled deeper into the hay. I ran my hand down his neck again. It was like I was stroking a big, black, dangerous lion. My fingers gently combed through his fur as my heart swelled with affection and something else—trust. I'd just had my first real conversation with this dog.

It was magic.

CHAPTER 5

Stupid Boy

ALTHOUGH DEEP DOWN I KNEW MY FAMILY LOVED ME, ONE of the reasons I ran away from home was because they didn't understand me at all. I was born with ADHD but back in the 1970s, no one knew much about it. In case you're wondering, it stands for Attention-Deficit-Hyperactivity-Disorder, and, I agree, it's a bloody mouthful.

So what's it like having ADHD? Well, for me it was like drinking a hundred cans of Coca-Cola a day. With that much energy fizzing around inside me, sitting still and concentrating were almost impossible. My ADHD drove everyone crazy. Even eating dinner with my family could quickly turn into a nightmare.

"Who's bloody jiggling the table?" Dad growled one night.

Without realizing it, my ADHD was making me fidget in my chair. My knees bounced, fingers tapped, and body wriggled. As a result, everything on the table trembled and rattled as though Garryowen was experiencing an earth tremor.

"Is this a joke? Whoever the hell it is, stop jiggling!" yelled Dad, thumping the table. Major and Rex slunk out of the kitchen fast. My brothers and sisters flicked me looks of annoyance. If they could sit the fuck still, why couldn't I?

I tried to get my body to behave, but before long, the table would start jiggling again and so did the sauce bottle, the milk container, glasses of water, the salt and pepper shakers. A few things even bumped over and fell onto the floor.

"Marcine! Mar-*cine!*" Mammy hissed, trying to get my attention. She could never pronounce my name properly.

Crack! Dad clipped me in the ear. "Your mother wants to speak to you. Stop fidgeting."

"Please take your elbows off the table, Marcine. Remember manners are important." I really wanted to please her, but before long my mind was racing away again and . . .

Crack! "Your mother said elbows off the table," Dad rumbled. "Use your brain and think." *Crack!* "And stop bloody fidgeting! I can't bloody digest my food with all your silly-bugger jumping and jiggling. Outside and wait. You can come back in when we've finished our meal in blessed peace."

I got used to waiting in our backyard with Major and Rex while everyone else in the family ate their dinner. Starving, I'd stand on my tip-toes to peer through the kitchen window. Then I'd start jumping up and down impatiently. To my family I must have looked like a human pogo stick.

Dad didn't care. "Get away from that window or I'll flog you!"

Strangely, when I was left alone with Major and Rex, my ADHD slowed right down and went to sleep. Within minutes I'd be calm and quiet. Why was that? Major, Rex, and I never argued. I did what I wanted and they followed me about like worried nannies. I constantly imagined them rolling their eyes to high heaven, saying to each other, *What a bloody nuisance of a pup. Why can't he just stop sticking his nose into everything?* If I began getting out-of-control hyper, the dogs didn't get angry or frustrated like humans. Instead, they went neutral, or moved slower. Often they turned their heads away and ignored me until I relaxed. If this didn't work, they simply went to sleep until I calmed down. I'd creep closer and curl up beside them. It was wonderful feeling all that super-hyperactive energy leave my body. No wonder I was drawn to these two kind, wise dogs.

ADHD caused other sorts of difficulties for me. Like the time I woke in the middle of the night feeling hungry. I tried to ignore it but my stupid stomach wouldn't let me. *Feed me, feed me, feed me!*

There was no chance ignoring that bloody dictator's voice. ADHD burnt up so much of my energy that I needed to eat the moment I got hungry or my stomach started devouring itself. Trouble was, I'd been forbidden on the pain of death from entering the kitchen after everyone went to bed. This was because I kept eating the food carefully put aside for breakfast and lunch the next day. I was infamous for it.

Cursing my stomach, I snuck downstairs to the kitchen. There was only one place to look for food: the bread bin on the counter. I slid back the lid and saw two loaves inside. One loaf was for breakfast, the other for school lunches, leaving absolutely none for my midnight snack. My fingers hesitated. Mammy was going to hit the roof in the morning, but what could I do? My stomach was making me demented. The fluffy white loaf closest to me seemed to be singing my name, calling me closer. My ten thieving fingers reached in and liberated it. It smelt so delicious. Perhaps a very small slice or . . . ?

An idea hit me. Very carefully, I sawed off the end of the loaf with the bread knife. *Nicely done, Martin. Now the tricky bit.* I gently pulled bits of the soft center out and popped them in my mouth. *Mmmm. Perfect.* I pulled bits of bread out faster and faster until my fingers reached in and touched only hard crust.

Jesus! I'd eaten *everything* inside the loaf. The stupid thing was now completely hollow. *Fuck, fuck, fuck.*

Don't panic, I told myself. *Just think.* What if I used a bit of jam to glue the end I'd cut off back on the rest of the loaf back? It was worth a try. Pretty inventive really. Once I'd done that I slid the thing back in the bread bin and closed the lid briskly. *La-la-la.* No one need ever know I'd been near it. I realized I was now desperately thirsty after eating all that bread. Of course there was tap water or . . .

I opened the fridge and saw that there was only one unopened bottle of milk left. Just my luck. It was obviously being saved for tomorrow's cereal and Dad's cup of tea.

God, how I love milk, I thought as my eyes flicked over the full bottle. I decided to make a deal with myself. I'd just limit myself to three *small* mouthfuls then re-fill the bottle with tap water. Who'd notice?

The trouble was the milk tasted *so* good going down my gullet that when I finally came up for air, there was . . . well . . . hardly any left. Bugger. When I filled the bottle to the brim with tap water it turned a strange watery color, but what the hell could I do about it now?

With a flourish, I put the bottle back in the fridge and banged the door shut. Out of sight, out of mind, problem expertly fixed, Mammy happy, blah-blah-blah . . .

Then it hit me. I was alone in the kitchen unsupervised. It was the perfect opportunity to hunt down the one substance I was absolutely forbidden to touch. *Sugar.* No joke, I was the world's worst sugar addict—so bad the family had to hide it from me. Now like a seasoned junkie, I started ransacking the kitchen for the sugar bag, hoping Mammy hadn't locked it in her jewelry box. I opened all the cupboards, looked in all the drawers, inside all the teapots, jars, and usual bastard hiding places. I finally flung open the cupboard under the sink and smiled.

There it was.

The tiniest corner of the sugar bag was peeping out from behind the drain pipe. I pulled it out in triumph and brought it over to the kitchen table. Digging deep into the bag with a spoon, I scooped some up and jammed it in my mouth.

The sugar exploded on my tongue. I always loved that first hit. The problem was knowing when to stop. After a second third, fourth, fifth, and sixth spoonful, lightning spread through my system, like I'd pumped rocket fuel into my body. I swear I even saw stars.

I went completely crazy, climbing onto the table, hopping on the kitchen chairs, bouncing off the walls. My body was going totally haywire. I finally had to run out the kitchen door, over the back wall, and up and down the street in my bare feet.

Must run laps around our block, I told myself. One lap, two, three. Nope, still not enough to use up my energy. I climbed over cars parked along the curb and zigzagged in and out of neighbors' gates.

Then with no warning, my blood sugar level dropped suddenly to zero. Now I could barely walk. I was teetering on the verge of a monster sugar crash.

"Bed," I muttered. Each step was a huge effort as I staggered through the gate and somehow managed to haul myself up the drain pipe to our bedroom.

"Fuck off, Martin," muttered Andrew sleepily and pushed me off the bed for being so hot and sweaty. I rolled to the floor with a thud and lay staring at the ceiling, panting. I'd survived another midnight snack . . . sort of.

Next morning, I was woken by screaming.

"Mick! Mick! Oh, my God! Vat has happened to ze bread! It's all hollow inside! Somevone has vandalized the bread."

Dad trudged up the stairs, belt wrapped around his knuckles. I knew what was coming next. *Whack! Whack! Whack!* At bedtime he banished me to the coal shed with Major and Rex. As I huddled with my blanket, I couldn't help crying a bit. *Wasn't fair.* Major and Rex sniffed me gently. They could smell how upset I was and stuck their long noses in past my arms to lick my face to soothe me. Eventually they lay down next to me sighing deeply. The shed smelt of stale Guinness, German Shepherds, and coal dust.

Listening to the dogs breathing heavily, I began to relax. This was the usual story. As soon as there were only dogs around me and no humans, I calmed right down. Major and Rex curled into huge warm balls and fell sleep. I snuggled between them, close to their thick, shaggy coats.

———

If you think having ADHD was bad enough at home, imagine what it was like for me at school. The classroom was a torture chamber for someone like me. My school, St. Patrick's, demanded kids to sit absolutely still at their desks. Yeah, good luck getting my ADHD to listen to *that* clever idea.

There was also a running battle to stop me from using my left hand to write. It was supposed to be the hand of the Devil, and, apparently even more sinful, it made your writing look messy. My greatest enemy, however, was the dreaded chalkboard. I *loathed* it with every atom of my body. Why the hell did no one else have a problem with it?

I'd peek around my desk to watch the other kids working quietly. They had no trouble sitting still. They understood all the words and numbers as soon as they appeared on the chalkboard and copied them down effortlessly. Shit, some kids were even *smiling*! That really weirded me out.

Things were so different for me. When I looked at the chalkboard, all the letters and numbers galloped off in different directions until I was sure there was evil magic contained in that chalkboard. Why would the thing unlock its secrets for everyone except me?

To make things worse, John and Andrew never had any problems learning at school. No one in our family did except me. Mammy had been at university reading economics when she met my father. She was genuinely bewildered why I couldn't read or write.

"Why, Marcine? Can't you try to concentrate more? What am I going to do with you?"

Dad said I was a bold little bastard looking for attention. "Your teachers obviously aren't hitting you hard enough."

The teachers had another name for it. "Faul, you're not bold. You're stupid." They had a remedy for it too. Like my father, they believed being lashed across the head with a leather belt helped make you more intelligent. It was simply a matter of whacking the stupidity out. I learned that schools housed some of the nastiest bullies in the world—and I'm not talking about the kids. I mean the teachers. The worst offenders at my school were Mr. Keeley and Mr. Rollins.

"Would Mr. Faul *please* open his book so he can join the rest of us?" That was Mr. Keeley, the most sadistic of all, on one typical day. "If it's not too much trouble, Faul?"

The class twisted in their chairs to stare at me. I glared at Mr. Keeley, hating him more and more. He held up a book. "This...is...a...book. It's for *reading*." He opened the book. "You...will...find...it...easier...if...you...open...it."

The class tittered nervously. I folded my arms and stared him straight in the eye. He didn't like that.

"Let me rephrase that," he sneered. "Would *Mr. Stupid* please do as I do. *Open* the book." He opened the book again. "And at least *pretend* to read it."

Self-respect demanded I fight back. He was such a nasty piece of work—a real vicious bully. I kept staring at him.

He gave a theatrical sigh. "Oh, dear. Looks like *Mr. Stupid* needs a lesson in civilized behavior." His face dropped suddenly close to mine. "Hold out your hand. Can you do that, Faul, or do I need to draw a diagram?"

The class tittered, this time more nervously. We all knew what was coming. I stared straight back at him, folded my arms tighter, and breathed in nice and steady to ready myself.

The class fell silent.

Keeley glared at me, then turned and walked back to his desk. With each step his shoes squeaked but this time no one giggled. He slid open his desk drawer and pulled out his favorite toy so everyone could see it. It was a twelve-inch leather strap with a slim lead center threaded through the middle. It was a blackjack. God knew where he'd got it from. He slipped the leather handle over his wrist.

He took a few practice swings through the air. Nobody else moved. *Okay, here it comes.* I straightened my shoulders and breathed out hard. No way was that weak bastard seeing fear in my eyes. I'd rather eat my own arm.

"Hand," he said, his eyes sparkling with pleasure. My arms stayed folded. "Oh, dear," he drawled. "*Mr. Stupid* is being rather quiet. Let's see if we can get some noise out of him." *Thud!* He started hitting me. *Thud! Thud! Thwack!* Each blow to my arms, back, and shoulders was full of blunt pain.

It was hard not to cry out. I bit my bottom lip so no cries escaped and concentrated on glaring straight back into his eyes so I could show him *exactly* how much I loathed him.

He blinked and his control began to slip. "Why the hell won't you make a damned noise?" he yelled. He began hitting me harder and faster until he realized even that wouldn't break me. When he finally stopped, he was panting hard. As he pushed back a lock of his greasy hair he yelled, "Get out! Straight to the headmaster's office! Before I *really* lose my temper!"

I'd won. Shoving back my chair, I held my head high and glanced around as I strolled out between the desks. No kids were laughing now. They were all bent over their books, desperately pretending to read. They knew as soon as I left the room, Keeley was going to take his frustration out on somebody else. Who was his next victim going to be?

❦

Such victories were rare. Most of the time, the teachers just ignored me. I must have been too exhausting to fight all the time. I felt completely isolated, trapped in a bubble while the rest of the class worked together as a team.

It baffled me why John and Andrew were able to get along when I couldn't. They'd get so annoyed with me. "For God's sake, just sit down and do your work," John would snap at me. "You're getting us into trouble, too."

The harder I tried to concentrate, the faster all those letters and numbers raced around the blackboard in a bewildering jumble. I couldn't read or write—and probably never would. The teachers continued to sigh and roll their eyes in irritation. Sarcasm poured out of their mouths like taps no one could turn off.

"Surely you can write your name by now?" drawled Mr. Keeley one day. "Even my most stupid students have managed that baby step. Perhaps we should change your name to Mr. *Ex-treme-ly* Stupid, because without a doubt, Faul, you're the most *stupid boy* I've ever met."

This generated more tittering from the class.

After that, he just called me "Stupid Boy."

Stupid Boy.

Keeley was right. If I couldn't even write my own name I must be stupid.

CHAPTER 6

Padraig O'Rourke's Barn

I DON'T KNOW WHAT WAS WORSE—GETTING DAILY BEATINGS from Mr. Keeley or having to steal my dinner from a trash bin, as I was now forced to do almost a year after I'd run away from home. Sometimes I wondered if "Stupid Boy" had gotten any smarter, but there I was going through the garbage at the Castletroy Estate when a car suddenly turned down the street towards me.

I looked around in panic. There was nowhere to hide except one place: under a parked van. The road was freezing against my soaking wet back. The car passed by, splashing icy water in my eyes.

After the car had gone, I crawled out again and looked down at myself. With all the mud and ice dripping off me, I was a real mess. I glanced back at the garbage can but was too depressed to keep looking through it. I'd rather go hungry tonight and just go back to my dogs.

Or was it time to admit defeat and go home? This was the first time in the last three months I'd even considered the idea. Without warning, homesickness hit me hard, and I had the sudden crazy urge to go home and peer through the window at my family. *Are you crazy, Martin?* Even the thought of a secret visit set my heart racing and my hands trembling. What if my father grabbed me? He'd lock me in my bedroom, bolt my window, and wield that belt like never before.

Worse, I was terrified of Mammy catching sight of me. I never stopped feeling guilt for the pain I had caused her. How the neighbors must have whispered among themselves after I ran away!

But as I trudged back along the railway towards Padraig's barn, I couldn't get the crazy idea out of my head. Just one peek through the front window. My feet carried me across frosty fields until I reached the Garryowen estate and through my family's front gate.

It was so weird being home again.

The curtains weren't drawn, so warm light spilled out of the living room window like an invitation. I forced my feet to step closer and raised my head cautiously to peer over the window sill. I caught my breath. It was surreal, like watching the perfect family on a TV show. My heart slammed hard against my ribs as I thought, *Look how happy everyone is!*

There was my mother sitting in an armchair. All I wanted to do was run inside, climb into her lap and hug her tight. I'd never seen her smiling like that! She was chatting happily to my sister and looked if a great weight had been lifted from her shoulders.

Then it dawned on me. *I* was the weight that had been lifted from her life.

There were my sisters and brothers lounging around on the carpet watching TV together. Everyone was laughing. Even Andrew and John looked so carefree.

This suddenly made me realize what a curse I had been on them. Once I left, Andrew and John were free to lead happy, normal lives. *My whole family was only a mess when I was around.*

I looked down at the concrete, desperately trying to keep the tears away. If I'd been normal, if I hadn't been stupid, I could be there with them. Being as happy as they were.

I helplessly peered back in. I could hardly believe it when I saw my father. Was that really him? He was smiling at the TV, making my eldest sister laugh with a joke. He looked ten years younger and was clearly sober. Now he'd give Cary Grant a good run for his money. No wonder Mammy was smiling.

I shivered. One thing was certain—I couldn't go back and mess up my family, not when I saw how happy they were without me.

⸻

By the time I made it back to Padraig's barn and climbed to the top of the loft, I felt completely overwhelmed. I lit a candle and saw the dogs were already asleep. They wagged their tails softly but didn't bother to get up.

I sank down in the hay. "Hi everyone," I said miserably. I knew I couldn't afford to get sad. These days I needed every scrap of energy just to survive. I'd better cheer myself up and fast. *You're okay, Martin. The dogs are your family now.*

"What I need is a hug," I said softly under my breath. Although I normally hated hugs, I really needed to know someone loved me on this dreary night. Shyly, I crawled across the hay to Mossy and looked down upon him fondly. "I'm so lucky to have you as a friend, boy." He was stretched out asleep, so I lay down facing him, trying not to disturb him too much.

I snuggled down next to him and breathed in his warm coat, the way I used to do with Major and Rex. He lifted his head slightly, saw it was me and flopped back down, closing his eyes.

It made me feel good how he trusted me. I put my arm gently over his shoulders, and after a slight hesitation, hugged him.

He dived away, nearly snapping my nose off.

"You stupid dog!" I yelled, sitting up. "Why the hell did you do that?"

Mossy looked over his shoulder at me as he padded off, dropped back into the hay, and curled up again.

"You've got to be kidding!" I said. All I wanted was a bloody hug. After all he was my *dog*. It was his job to be hugged and damn well enjoy it. Determined, I crawled towards him on my hands and knees. He sat up and then deliberately turned his head away and held the pose.

Please leave me alone, he was saying loud and clear in dog language. It was like a slap in the face. Now even my own dog was rejecting me.

"Stop bloody telling me to go away!" I yelled, my temper rising fast. I couldn't remember ever feeling this hurt by a dog. Tonight of all nights when the whole world felt like such a cold and lonely place, my best friend was letting me down. "Why are you acting so weird and horrible towards me?" I asked.

Mossy yawned noisily. *Just chill out and relax,* he was saying firmly in dog language.

"I won't bloody calm down!" I snapped. "All I want is a hug from you!"

The other dogs started sitting up sleepily. They took one look at my face and started turning their heads away too until they all looked like statues, their body language all saying the same thing: *Please leave us alone.*

"Is this some sort of stupid joke?" I thumped the hay with clenched fists. "All I do with you dogs is give, give, give. It's time you gave me back something. *A simple hug.* Is that too much to ask?"

I scrambled towards the dogs. They yawned, turned their heads away from me, then darted out of reach.

"I don't give a shit whether you want to hug me or not," I snapped, "You're all hugging me, or you can leave this barn tonight!" By now the dogs were growling and snapping as they dodged out of my outstretched hands. Realizing how crazy I was behaving, I sat down, panting hard. Then a strange thing started happening. The dogs began playing among themselves. Within seconds, their play got rougher, and scuffles broke out with lots of harsh snarling and snapping. Red and Pa's wrestling game was quickly getting serious. They leapt high at each other, putting their paws around each other's necks and biting sharply.

It suddenly hit me why these dogs didn't want to hug me: *To dogs, a hug is like a fight-hold.*

No wonder Mossy freaked out when I tried to hug him while he was half-asleep. He thought I was trying to play-wrestle him while he was vulnerable. As for the rest of the dogs, they hadn't run away because they disliked me. They simply didn't want to wrestle with me when I was in such a strange, intense mood.

"Okay, you can calm down now," I said. The dogs stopped play-fighting and looked at me warily. "Just a stressful day. I'm alright now. Sorry I freaked you out."

When they didn't seem reassured, I yawned slowly and sleepily, gently closing my eyes. The dogs' taut energy instantly relaxed. They shook themselves.

I tried to get my head around what I'd just discovered. "Don't be stupid, Martin," I said out loud. "Everyone knows dogs *love* being hugged. Dogs have been hugged in every dog movie you've ever seen. They love it! What about all those dogs on TV? What about Lassie?" Yet I couldn't get the idea that dogs think hugging is a sign of aggression rather than affection out of my head. As I had done before, I felt the need to test my theory, so first I got the dogs in a much calmer mood. Fifteen minutes of yawning had them relaxed even to the point that I was able to stroke them all affectionately.

Yep, they trusted me again. First I tried Pa. I slid my arms around him affectionately. "Good boy, fella. What do you think of this?" Pa energetically licked my face. "Yuck!" I released him fast, wiping my mouth in disgust. "Why'd you do that? You know I hate it when you lick my mouth." I looked closely at his facial expression. His panting was heavier than normal and his smile was too exaggerated. He seemed to be *grimacing*, not grinning. I hugged him again. He leaned away from me within the circle of my arms, his head swiveling as far from me as he could. In other words, he was telling me to leave him alone. When I kept hugging him, he dived in to lick me hard on the mouth. I guessed that licking someone on the face was Pa's way of saying, *Hey! Give me some personal space, please.* I'd seen him do it to other dogs plenty of times until they left him alone. I stopped hugging him, and instantly he stopped trying to dart in and lick me in that annoying way.

Next, I tried Missy. "Come here, darling," I said softly. She popped out of my arms like a Jack-in-the-box when I hugged her gently. Each time I tried she bounced out or wriggled free. "Obviously you don't like hugs either."

"Hello, fella," I said as I moved in on Fergus. When I slid my arms around him, he stayed perfectly still—unnaturally still. Then he started panting heavily and grimacing the way Pa had.

Very slowly, he turned his head away from me. "Sorry, boy," I apologized as I let him go. Once free, he shook his whole body. There was that stupid body shake again. Why the hell did the dogs keep doing *that*? I decided to try a different technique with Fergus. This time I slid an arm around his shoulder so we were sitting side by side like the best of pals. "What do you think, Fergus?" I asked. "Do you like this any better or hate it?" Fergus clearly disliked it and pretended to chew at a flea at the base of his tail. This clever maneuver slipped him straight out from under my arm. I laughed. "Very smooth." I tried it again, and he made the same maneuver.

Now it was Red's turn. When I hugged him, he bounced straight up and bumped my chin so hard that I fell back, releasing him instantly. "Ouch! You bugger! You did that deliberately." On a second try he bumped me so hard, my eyes watered. "Nope. Guess you don't like being hugged either," I said, rubbing my throbbing chin. "Geez, did you have to hurt me that much?"

I looked at Blackie, and he just growled deep in his throat. "Yep. Guess that's a no." Having no wish to get my face ripped off, I went back to Mossy, my first test subject.

"Let's see what you think of being hugged, boy." At first he enjoyed it—or seemed to. He leaned against me, looking up with a really soppy expression on his face.

"Well," I said in surprise. "Maybe I'm wrong." I kept hugging Mossy gently, but then he started getting restless within my arms. When I didn't release him, his play got rougher. A few times his teeth grazed my neck and ears as he kept whipping his head around playfully. He bumped my nose hard. Worse, he licked me without warning right between the lips so his tongue slid right inside my mouth. *Ugh!* I gave up. Exhausted, I flopped back in the hay, blew out the candle, and pulled a thick layer of hay over me like a blanket. My mind was whirling.

What about all those cute TV ads? And all those Hollywood movies where people hugged their dogs? I'd grown up with those images. The dogs had looked so unbelievably happy—or were they? I tried to remember their expressions exactly. Were the dogs on the screen grinning with happiness? Or were they actually panting from stress or grimacing to show how uncomfortable they felt?

Another thought hit me. Had they actually been trained to sit still and accept being hugged by human actors? It was crazy but all my instincts were whispering I was right—that dogs think of hugs as fight holds. Playful or serious, it wasn't a sign of affection to them like it was for us humans, yet we still kept hugging them. *Poor dogs,* I thought just before nodding off. *What else are you trying to tell us?*

CHAPTER 7

Outsiders

MY INTERACTIONS WITH THE DOGS HAD ME THINKING QUITE a bit about my past interactions with people. Why did humans seem to have such a hard time understanding and accepting each other? Why was my family always treated like outsiders just because my mammy was German? All these questions made me remember the day local hostility for us finally boiled over during an international soccer match.

Mammy was watching it with us kids on TV. We all cheered when her beloved West German team won. "That vas *vonderful!*" she laughed. "Such skilled, beautiful playing. Vell done, Germany! There will be such a party there tonight!"

Our father was away on transport maneuvers with the army, and our older brother and sisters were out somewhere else. For once we younger kids were ecstatic to have her to ourselves.

Suddenly from outside the house came loud chanting. "Nazis! Nazis! Nazis!" Boys were walking towards our house, shouting abuses. Everyone in Garryowen who'd been watching the important match was furious that their favorite team had lost. As Mammy was the only German in our neighborhood, the local kids must have decided to make her their target.

It didn't help that the sports commentators had been openly derogatory about the West German team, whipping up public outrage. Andrew, John, and I knew how much Germans were still disliked even though World War II was in the distant past. Kids devoured comics and everyone knew who the good and bad guys were. Good guys were instantly recognizable. They had strong jaws and straight gazes and American or British accents. Bad guys had cruel eyes and German accents. We three were fiercely protective of Mammy and her German blood. How could we not admire her? She held our world together with her heart and soul, struggling every day with tasks that would fell ten men.

The yelling outside grew louder. "Nazis! Nazis! Nazis!" Fourteen boys had gathered across the road and sat on the low wall opposite our house. "Nazis go back home!" one boy yelled then howled. The others cheered.

"Please," Mammy begged. "Ignore them. If we stay inside, they'll get bored and go home."

The voices got louder and more raucous. "Hey! Nazi bitch! Why don't you go back to Germany and take your creepy Hitler kids with you!" One stone then another hit our house. Our sisters ran to Mammy and hid in her arms. More stones followed. The chants grew louder and fiercer. We glared helplessly through the window at them.

"Please don't go out there! They'll hurt you!" begged Mammy.

We looked at her.

"Don't listen to them. I'm not a Nazi. You know how much I hate them. They destroyed our country, our culture. That's vy I left Germany as a young woman—to escape the shame and horror."

A big stone crashed against our front door.

"Come out and fight us, you freak clones!" yelled one kid, louder than the rest.

John, Andrew, and I looked at each other. As usual it seemed like the whole world was out to get us. We'd protect Mammy and our sisters. How dare those cowards stand out there in a crowd and yell abuses at our poor mother. Would we stay inside and hide? No way. "No one threatens Mammy," said John quietly. We nodded, our secret motto running through our minds. *If we fight, we fight to the end. No one gets left behind.*

We were gone before Mammy could stop us. We ran to the coal shed where our hurling sticks were stored then raced back through the house, banged open the front door, and flew over the threshold, launching ourselves right into the rabble of fourteen yelling, jeering kids. Right in front were Malarky, Ger, and Nane, three of the worst bullies on the Garryowen estate.

Smash! I felt my hurling stick make contact with Malarky's shins. He grunted with pain and doubled over. *Crack!* My hurley flew upwards, making fine contact with his head. *Fuck!* Someone landed me a good punch on the cheek, so I jabbed him in the eye with the end of my stick.

The battle grew in ferocity, reaching the point that everything wash appening so fast, all we could do was stay on our feet and do as much damage to our enemies as possible. John and Andrew were making their hurleys sing. As usual when we fought together, we fought well. There's nothing like having two courageous brothers fighting at your side, knowing they're just as staunch as you are.

By the time the battle died down, everyone was exhausted, but it was clear we triplets had won. We were standing—our enemies were not.

Malarky, the bully leader, crawled to his feet. "Come on," he ordered his two bully friends. "Let's get out of here." He spat on the ground in my direction and slunk off. Ger and Nane got up and followed, all three nursing bloody wounds as they limped away. "I'll get you, Faul!" Malarky yelled over his shoulder at me. He was fuming because I'd made him look like a hopeless fighter. Me, the stupid, skinny kid at school and the runt of the triplets, I had flogged him in front of everyone.

"Cowards!" screamed Andrew after the three boys.

They yelled back threats but we just laughed, so they kept walking.

The rest of us—the remaining eleven boys and we three triplets—sank down on the footpath. We were panting hard, wiping bloody noses and cuts, and wincing as we examined our battle wounds.

A little mongrel belonging to Seamus O'Keefe wandered over and licked his bleeding nose. The boy was lying flat on his back on the pavement. "Piss off, Mickey," he croaked in exhaustion.

A door slammed open down the street. Without warning, Mr. McGowan marched straight up the pavement towards us, his eyes shooting sparks in all directions. He was a neighbor who usually wouldn't say boo to a goose. He glared at each of us. "Why are you kids trying to murder each other?" he snarled. "Fools! You should be fighting the *English*, not each other. We're all Irish here—and don't you bloody forget it!"

Dazed, we watched him stomp back down the pavement towards his front gate and disappear inside, the front door slamming behind him.

Michael from next door hung his head in shame. "Sorry, Faullies. Please apologize to your mam for us."

The other boys nodded in agreement. "Sorry," each said.

Michael shook his head ruefully then held out his hand. "Friends?"

John, Andrew, and I looked at each other. "Yeah," said John taking Michael's hand. "Friends." He gazed around fiercely. "But you'd better tell everyone to leave Mammy alone. She's not some Nazi and neither are we."

We all shook hands warily, Celtic honor restored.

Only those three sly cowards had slunk off without apologizing.

Next morning we found a big blue swastika that Malarky, Ger, and Nane had painted on the front of our house in the middle of the night. It seemed we now had three more enemies to worry about.

—◦—

We triplets weren't the only outsiders in Garryowen, of course. Outsiders fascinated me because they had such different opinions from everyone else. Their unusual way of looking at the world always opened new doors in my mind.

The best known outsiders in Garryowen were the gypsies who lived at Rhebogue. My brothers and I loved wandering around their camp. The old gypsy ladies were just as fascinated by us. "You three are very *special*. Do you know that?" they said, cupping our faces and kissing us gently on the foreheads. "There you go, loves—a kiss for each of ye. You're now under the protection of the gypsies."

They were different in other ways. They smoked wooden pipes and sat in old car seats pulled up around the main camp fire. Some families still lived in traditional brightly painted wooden caravans; most had modern caravans pulled by station wagons.

What you noticed most about the gypsies was their gold. In their teeth, hanging from their wrists and necks, and worn on every finger. Most of this beautiful jewelry was also studded with precious stones—diamonds, rubies, emeralds, and sapphires. It was like they'd gone on holiday to Aladdin's cave and brought back enormous handfuls of treasure as tourist souvenirs.

Boy, I had fierce arguments with those ten thieving fingers of mine, but even I was too scared to steal from the gypsies. It was said if you stole gold from a gypsy then you were cursed for life. Ha! The last thing I needed was *more* bad luck, so my fingers left the gypsy gold alone.

I really liked and respected their head man, Charlie Clarke. He had ringlets which fell in grey clouds to his shoulders. His face was like a piece of worn leather. He was in charge of everyone in the gypsy camp and all the animals too. He was always tough on me about not annoying the camp animals with endless pats. "Leave that dog alone," he'd say. "Can't you see how much you're annoying it? Look at its ears. It's telling you how much of a pain in the arse you're being."

Charlie Clarke's gypsy camp was such an enticing place to flirt with danger. For a long time my thieving fingers absolutely *craved* to borrow one of his gypsy horses. Late one night, I finally persuaded John and Andrew to sneak out and steal three of Charlie's horses for a midnight ride.

"Come on, it'll be great fun," I said, sitting on the end of the bed.

My brothers stared at me in dismay. "You've got to be kidding," said Andrew at last. "Charlie'll skin us alive."

John shook his head. "You're crazy. Go back to bloody sleep."

"Ha! Are you scared . . . or are you coming?" It was our own private taunt, and it always worked.

Reluctantly, my brothers joined me in pulling on shoes. Still in our pajamas, we shimmied down the pipe outside our bedroom and belted down the road towards the gypsy camp.

"Isn't this great?" I whispered gleefully.

We snuck past the camp hoping the gypsy dogs wouldn't start barking. A real Irish mist was rising from the grass, touching us all over with its soft, damp fingers.

My blood sang through my body as we entered the field where the horses were kept. We couldn't see a thing, so we had to feel our way forward with our feet and our outstretched hands.

"Listen," I murmured softly, "or we'll never find them in the dark."

"I can hear one over this way," hissed back John. "That's mine."

"I'll grab this one over here," whispered Andrew, moving off.

I kept tramping forward into the pitch-black darkness, my hands stretching out in front of me, my ears straining. I knew there must be at least nine horses grazing somewhere in the field. I heard a sharp snort and before I could blink, hooves thundered straight for me in the pitch dark.

We must have spooked the horses. Now they're stampeding right for us.

In a flash, I remembered how Charlie Clarke stopped the horses and sent his familiar words out into the darkness, "Bewisht. Halt. Woo-stand. Stand with ye, hosses. Stand and be gentle there."

On either side of me, I heard my brothers taking up the same steady refrain. Together we held our ground, which was shaking beneath our feet.

This is it. We're gonna die.

Then there was the deafening sound of the huge horses skidding and sliding towards us. My heart kicked back to life when they stopped. *Jesus, that was close!* I felt the delicate touch of their upper lips moving over my body as they tried to smell who I was.

It was then that I remembered Charlie Clarke's words of wisdom. "It's the ultimate truth test when ye blow into a hoss's nose," he'd told me countless times before. "Y'know why? 'Cause the smell of yer breath doesn't lie." He'd pointed his pipe at me. "A hoss can smell exactly what yer intentions are—whether yer kind or cruel. It can always smell the truth in yer heart."

I blew gently into the horse's nostrils, trying to feel as calm and kind as I could. "Whist, hoss. Stand with ye," I said again. On either side of me, I could hear Andrew and John also settling the horses. "You ready?" I called out softly. If we were safe, the adventure was back on again.

"Ready," was their reply.

I'd ridden plenty of gypsy horses but never at night and *never* without Charlie's permission. I grabbed a handful of shaggy mane and hauled myself upwards. For a moment my nose was full of mist-damp shaggy mane. Then my leg swung over its back and I was up.

We didn't need saddles, bridles, or reins. Not after all the times we'd ridden with the gypsy kids. They'd taught us how to balance ourselves bareback. I wrapped my fingers tight in the horse's mane, dug my heels in its huge sides, and bit back a whoop as it lurched forward.

The huge horse went into a slow canter and then got steadily faster until we were galloping wildly across the field in the pitch dark. What did we care about falling and breaking our necks? Not a damn.

My heart sang. The horse snorted happily beneath me as its huge hooves ate up the ground. My brothers and I were like

Celtic warriors two thousand years ago, heading out on a raid to steal our enemies' cattle.

All I wanted was to throw back my head and howl. This was much more exciting than hurling!

Then out of the mist a man appeared. A torch shining upwards illuminated his face eerily. It was Charlie.

The horses skidded to a halt, just as terrified as we were. Everyone knew how forbidden it was to ride Charlie's horses without his permission. I couldn't tear my eyes away from his face. I'd never seen him so expressionless. He didn't even have his blackthorn stick with him; instead, he was carrying his dreaded whip.

"Get off that hoss," he said softly. The quieter Charlie got, the scarier he became.

I slid straight off the horse's back, desperate excuses already pouring from my mouth. "Hiya, Charlie. You won't believe this but we just found these horses being chased up the road by a real mean dog and . . ." As soon as my toes touched the ground, the horse took off as fast as its legs could carry it. It was no fool.

Charlie was tapping that whip in the palm of his hand. "You'll have to lie better than that," he said calmly.

Now my brothers joined me, standing in front of him, lying our heads off about rescuing the horses from a savage dog.

"Right," he said when we finished talking. "You know the deal." His whip lashed swiftly and furiously over us until we were hopping in agony, yelping in pain. God, he knew how to make that whip sting. At last he stopped. "There you go. It's done." He brought out his pipe and smoked while letting us cry in peace until he said calmly, "Enough."

We rubbed our eyes with the back of our sleeves.

He looked at each of us keenly. "You know those hosses have to work hard tomorrow. Can't have ye three young fools racing them around, exhausting them. Especially in the dark. Idiots! If they'd fallen and broken their legs, they'd have to be shot. Happens easy as *that*." His fingers snapped sharp as if breaking a twig. "Problem with most people when it comes to animals is that nobody thinks of the *consequences*." Charlie gave us a steady look to make sure we understood, then jerked his chin in the direction of the estate. "Go on with ye. Get home and we'll not talk of this again."

We crawled into bed painfully that night. I heard my brothers next to me sigh in exhaustion and settle down to sleep, but I kept picturing those magnificent gypsy horses tripping in the dark and breaking their legs. For hours I lay unable to sleep, Charlie's words ringing in my ears.

"Nobody thinks of the consequences."

Jack McNamara was a completely different character than the gypsies. He was an eccentric outsider living on the Garryowen estate who fixed lawn mowers for a living. He taught me to ask questions about everything. He was extremely proud to be Irish. His house was filled floor to ceiling in every room with thousands of books.

"What are all these stupid things for?" I asked, wrinkling my nose at their moldy smell.

He smiled grimly and made a grandiose gesture at the bookcases. "Inside these books is *everything* about how to bring down the British Empire."

I looked at the books, unimpressed. "You're crazy, Jack."

"Aha! Scoff, boy, but believe me, the answer's somewhere in there." He patted a book like it was a loyal dog. "Yep. One day I'll find out the answer in these history books and *wham*! That bloody bastard British Empire will come crashing down and release Ireland from its colonial grip!"

He was fascinating to listen to. He told me about the downfall of the Assyrian, Babylonian, Egyptian, Phoenician, Persian, Chinese, Indian, Mongol, Greek, Minoan, Mayan, Etruscan, Roman empires until blah-blah-blah, my ears were ringing.

These conversations always ended with me wiping Jack's spittle off my face. "Settle down, Jack," I'd say. "It's all a long time ago. You're losing it, Jack. Come on. Settle down. You're starting to freak me out." The idea of me calming someone else down for a change was funny.

One evening he got extremely upset while talking about Queen Victoria. "Drug dealer! That's what she was—and the rest of the English rich! They got the whole of China deliberately hooked on *opium*! Brought the evil stuff in from India. How *vile* is that?" he yelled. "Turned millions of Chinese into addicts just to *milk* them of their money!"

His spittle misted over my face and I wiped it off with my sleeve. "Settle down, Jack."

He gestured in the air wildly. "In fact, Queen Victoria was one of the *biggest* bloody drug dealers ever born. Forget your Columbian cartels and drug lords! *Buckingham Palace* is nothing but a massive drug dealer's *mansion*! You don't get to build and decorate a house that big by selling bloody *tea* to English housewives!"

"It's okay. Settle down, Jack."

He started pacing the room. "Christ! When I start talking about bloody Buckingham Palace, I need a bloody drink," he said grimly. He stomped out of the room, brought back a bottle, and banged it on the table.

I instantly recognized what it was and felt my eyes widen and my heart quicken. *Poteen.* Home-made Irish moonshine. "Go on, Jack. Give us a taste," I said eagerly. I'd only ever drunk Guinness, whisky, and cider before, never the legendary poteen. It was supposed to be the most dangerous and manliest of drinks—even my father respected it.

Jack shook his head. "No way. Your parents would skin me alive."

"What? Stop kidding around. I've been drinking for years. Give us a drink, Jack." I bugged him relentlessly until he gave in.

"Okay, but you'll need to shut up," he snapped. "I need to concentrate."

I reached greedily for the bottle but before my fingers got near, his fingers snapped like a vice around my wrist. He glared. "Sit down, fool," he said. "If you get this next bit wrong, you can go *blind*. Maybe die." Focusing fiercely on the bottle, he picked up his lighter and held it carefully over the neck. Very slowly he began to undo the lid, then paused. His eyes met mine.

Yeah, yeah, I thought. *Just pour the bloody stuff.*

"You have to check the color of the flame before you drink a drop. Have to see if it's safe." He clicked his lighter and we both watched the long flame stretch smoothly upwards.

He licked his lips and recited, "If it's red, you'll soon be dead. If it's blue, it won't kill you." The flame flickered, then blazed blue.

Shouldn't kill us then.

Jack raised his eyes to mine and smiled grimly. "After you, young fella." He slid the bottle across the table towards me.

"I'll open the bottle but you pour your own. I'm not being charged with manslaughter. Anything happens to you, I'll deny everything."

I reached out and slowly poured the clear liquid into the glass. The fumes alone could have stripped paint. *Ugh!* I blew outwards fast to fight the vicious smell, quickly raised the glass to my lips, and threw the contents straight down the back of my throat.

Oh, fuck.

My mouth, throat, and head exploded like I had been hit with napalm. I ran outside and vomited violently on Jack's neatly mown lawn. After that, I collapsed to the ground, my face mashed in the grass.

Oh, God.

The backyard spun. If I wanted to survive, I mustn't move.

Jack McNamara's voice cut through the night, distorting muzzily. "There you go, young fella. They always say when you drink poteen, you share your first drink with the Devil. So what d'yer think?"

After I vomited lavishly once more, it was clear the Devil and I should never meet over a glass of poteen again.

CHAPTER 8

The Garryowen Horse Fair

LIVING ON MY OWN FORCED ME TO COME UP WITH WAYS TO earn money so I could feed myself. I was in a hurry to get to the Garryowen Horse Fair. Finally I had a chance to earn some money to buy some hot food! However, there I was still stuck on the railway line, wondering what to do with the bloody dogs.

They were milling around my legs, begging to be included in the adventure. Sometimes the six of them were like balls and chains around my ankles, dragging at my freedom.

They looked up with their pleading eyes. *Pleeeease take us with you.*

The bastards would tear your heartstrings right out of you if they could get away with it. I hardened my heart. "Sorry, no way you're coming with me today. Not around horses." I turned my head, closed my eyes, and breathed slowly to emphasize my message. Then I crossed my arms to show how much I meant it. In other words, I was using body language to tell them, *Respect my wishes, and leave me alone, please.* As usual, it worked perfectly. The dogs gave me one last beseeching look before melting away.

The fair was held on the Garryowen Horse Green, which was on top of a huge mound of earth beside the Garryowen estate. This mound had once been an ancient king's burial chamber. It was so big it was like a vast hill covered in grass with a top as flat as a dinner plate.

I ran fast through the early morning mist. My feet sped up as I heard the familiar sounds of the horse fair. Old cars pulling creaking horse trailers through mud. Frightened horse squealing. Irritated stamping coming from rattling trucks. Men coughing on morning cigarettes. I hurried through the cars and trailers to find who I was looking for.

Chance Casey.

It was said that he was a gypsy who'd stopped travelling and settled down in Garryowen. Now he was the best horse broker in the district. My eyes raked the milling crowd for him.

Horse brokers were an old tradition in Ireland, and Chance was one of the best. He helped people buy and sell horses using secret hand signals and was important because he stopped the horse fair from turning into a one big furious brawl. There were other horse brokers, of course, but Chance Casey was one of the most respected.

"Morning, Mr. Casey," I said to his back.

He slowly turned around. He was still skinny and bent over and was wearing his familiar brown tweed jacket, hob-nailed boots, flat cap, and pants so worn they shone. His head was still tipped downwards but now he shook out his match and puffed on his pipe to get it going before slowly raising his eyes to mine.

Jesus. I winced. As usual he was carrying a real mother of a hangover. His eyes were so red, they looked like they'd been dipped in blood. They fell back to looking on the ground. That's where he usually looked.

"'Tis you," he muttered in his fast gypsy accent. "Yer be wantin' a job then?" His red eyes never left the tuft of grass at his feet.

"Aye, sir," I said eagerly. "Really need the money. Can I say you recommend me?"

"Aye."

"Thank you, sir!" I took off into the crowd. With Chance's backing, I should be able to get a few jobs holding horses for owners. There were maybe two hundred men milling around me and three hundred horses. A few kids were running wild—farmers' and gypsy kids mostly, but also a few local strays like me. All around me was a sea of male voices—everyone talking, muttering, whispering, and shouting about only one thing: horses. I kept an eagle eye out for anyone needing help.

Normally you wouldn't catch me near so many people. But this crowd was different. It was made up of farmers, dealers, and gypsies from outside Garryowen. Skinny kid like me slipping through the crowd? No one here cared. All this lot cared about was making the best horse deal they could, which suited me just fine.

Stop gawking, start hustling, I told myself, as I walked straight up to a man and his three fat sons unloading a cob from a horse truck. "Hold your horse for you, sir?"

The man glanced down at me. "On yer way. Don't be annoying me." He rudely turned his back while his three fat sons smirked.

Hmmm. Lovely family of pigs.

My next target was a thin, nasty looking man backing a Piebald mare out of a rusty horse trailer.

"Hold your horse for you, sir?"

He snaked around so quickly I had to take a step backwards. Before I could blink, two men appeared at his side. The man holding the horse narrowed his eyes and spat near my boots. "Don't know yer. Piss orf."

My stomach rumbled. Since I was so desperate for money to buy breakfast, I didn't budge. "Chance Casey sent me over," I said hopefully.

"Don't deal with no Chance. Piss orf." The three men eyed me suspiciously until I walked away.

Geez. What did you think I was going to do? Steal one of your horse's legs while you weren't looking?

My third target looked more promising. Here was a man holding a horse by its lead rope. The horse was a big, muscled Piebald with a huge, shaggy mane that looked freshly combed and brushed. The man looked even more anxious than I was as he stood on tip-toes to look over the crowd.

Excellent. La-la-la. I put on my most respectful face and hurried up to him. "Chance Casey sent me over. Any chance I can hold your horse, sir?"

Flustered, the man glanced down at me and then peered back over the crowd. "Ah, well, if you know Chance, suppose I can trust you." He stood on tip-toes again. "Fellow over there says he's interested in buying my horse. Must grab him before he spends his money elsewhere."

Yippee, I quietly rejoiced. *First job of the day.*

He went to hand me the rope but then hesitated, noticing how feral I looked with bits of hay stuck in my hair and my old, tattered clothes.

I smiled reassuringly and said, "Chance says I'm an excellent worker." It was only half a lie.

Reluctantly, he handed me the rope. Before I could blink, his finger started bossily pointing all over the place like a demented clock. "Now *this* is a very valuable animal. Don't be letting him eat *this* grass over here. And keep him from *that* cranky mare over there. I've seen her kick out a few times, especially at *that* nuisance of a gelding over there. Hold the rope like *this* and mind yer don't spook him. Just stand right *here* in this exact spot nice and quiet."

A fussy owner. Bor-ing. "Yes, sir. Not a problem, sir. Swear to God I won't, sir."

At last he hurried off with a worried frown still on his face. His horse glanced at me then dropped his head and went back to cropping grass.

"Okay for you. I wish I could eat free grass all day," I muttered. The horse flicked an ear lazily at me.

The crowd swelled around us. There was a lot of stamping and whinnying from irritated horses, sick of being jammed too close together and held by lead ropes when they wanted to wander off and eat the much longer grass in peace.

Meanwhile some men laughed and others whispered. Everywhere I looked, there were darting eyes and strange pockets of bad energy. Horse fairs always had an undercurrent of slyness, probably because so much money was involved.

I felt my ADHD starting to come alive around all this slyness, tension, and aggression. My fingers started to tremble, my feet started to jiggle, and my stomach started cramping with nerves.

The horse looked at me uneasily. *Anything we have to worry about?* he seemed to say.

A man behind my horse cursed. Another one jostled me rudely as he shoved past, enjoying how easily he could bump a skinny kid off balance.

I stroked the big horse's neck to reassure myself. "Whist, hoss. Whist." Charlie Clarke's way of speaking to horses always helped calm me down too. This huge animal was humming with calming energy. I could feel it beneath my palm. Horses were like big sponges soaking up my nervous energy. Even better, they seemed to neutralize all the bad energy swirling through a crowd before it could infect me. *Thanks, horse. Appreciate it.*

The owner returned with his prospective buyer, who proceeded to walk quietly walked around the horse, looking it over carefully.

My stomach rumbled. *Come on, come on,* I thought. *The thing's perfectly okay. Four feet, a head, a tail. Just buy the damned thing so I can go eat.*

"Bit thin on the shoulders," the buyer said at last.

"Maybe, but he's strong and willing," said the seller.

The buyer shook his head doubtfully. "Looks a bit weary for what I'm wanting. Need him to pull a big coal four-wheeler. To be honest, I'm looking for something with more spirit than this."

The seller puffed out his chest. "Spirit? He's got enough for six horses." He spun around to me. "Jump up and show this man some paces, young fella." Then he threw me up on the horse's bare back and whispered in my ear, "Make it impressive and I'll slip you something extra."

My legs dangled down on either side of the horse's big muscled back as the rope tied around its nose was quickly looped into reins and thrown to me. I clicked my tongue. "Go on. Whoop! Whoop!" I dug my heels into the horse's side to get it moving. It lurched forward. Poor thing was sluggish as an old rusty truck. *Time to do my job.* I made a great fuss of pretending to hold him back as I kicked him into a bouncy trot. "Whoa, sir! He's a bit much for me. He's dying to gallop! Shall I let him go, sir?"

The seller winked at me and his voice rose in excitement. "Better not, young fella. You'll never hold him back if he decides to bolt. Wants to go like the wind! Look at him! Rein him in! *Rein him in!*"

I played my part, acting like a cowboy on a spirited mustang. "Ooh, plenty of feisty blood in him, sir! He's dying to cut loose and run off. Get ready if he bolts!" I made a big deal of reining him in. The horse stopped dead like an old truck run out of diesel. I gave him one last nudge behind the shoulder blades and he pranced a bit more on the spot. Then I slid off him fast before he yawned and went to sleep on his feet.

The buyer eyed me suspiciously, but he was interested. He walked to the seller and murmured a price in his ear. The seller frowned, scratched his head, and banged his blackthorn stick against his boots in frustration. He was clearly not being offered the price he wanted.

My noisy stomach was frantic. *Come on. Come on. Buy the damned thing before I starve!*

The two men started bargaining hard. Then there was silence followed by more scratching of heads, more banging sticks on boots. They had come to a deadlock. "Will we call in Chance Casey? Bring him in to fix the deal?"

"Agreed. Call him over."

The call went through the crowd. "Chance! You're needed over here!" The request was shouted from group to group.

Chance wandered over, his red eyes glued to the grass. "Aye?"

"We need a fixer," said the seller.

Chance nodded. He walked closer to the seller and listened hard as the man muttered fast in his ear, their eyes never leaving the ground. Then Chance walked over to the buyer. Their eyes never left the ground as he listened again. A rough price was agreed.

I had to zip my mouth shut so I didn't start screaming, "Just hurry up before my stomach devours itself!"

Now they were down to the secret handshakes. I didn't really know what went on inside those lightly clasped hands, but I'd been told they were negotiating a price in secret. One tap of a finger on a palm meant one price. Two taps was a higher price, and so on.

The crowd gathered to witness the ferocious negotiating. Chance Casey's face was totally inscrutable. There were no clues there.

The seller kept banging his blackthorn stick in frustration. The buyer kept frowning at his horse. Chance kept walking between the two of them, clasping their hands to secretly reveal new price bids. Finally! The price was agreed! Hallelujah!

It was time to seal the deal. The buyer and seller clasped hands.

Chance placed one hand above their clasped hands and one hand below. He moved their hands in a slow, bouncing shake once, twice, three times. Chance stood back as each man spat on his palm then clapped it in a smooth, sliding way against the other man's palm in both directions. Once. Twice. The deal was done.

The spit was symbolic. *The truth from my tongue honors this deal.*

Even the cash for the horse was exchanged out of sight. The roll of money was slipped inside a clasped handshake to avoid nosy eyes. Chance had his money passed to him in another handshake. He nodded respectfully to both men and the crowd. Job well done.

Then the call went up again. "Chance! You're needed over here to fix a deal. Chance! Over here." He wandered off, head down, red eyes glued to the grass as usual.

The seller flipped me two coins which I caught, kissed, and slipped into my pocket. "Thank you, sir!"

He handed the horse's rope over to his new owner.

I stroked the horse's powerful neck as I murmured in his ear, "Hope you go to a nice home, boy." Then I was off to St. John's Square in Garryowen where one of my favorite places in the world was waiting—Ford's Fish and Chip Shop. Best food in the universe.

I ran full tilt towards the door, skidded to a walk, and groaned. *Oh, Hell!* There was already a queue of nine customers. The line moved slowly but I was nearly there when my eyes widened in horror as I realized who the woman was in front of me. Mrs. McCarty! *No, no! Doom!*

"Now good afternoon to you, Mrs. McCarty," said Mr. Ford, smiling in welcome. "What can I do for you?"

"Hello," replied Mrs. McCarty. "Hope you've got a pencil handy because you'll never remember such a long order off the top of your head. Bit of a big family we are. Ah, well, God's will, I suppose." I watched in dread as she pulled out a very long piece of paper from her handbag.

"Now, let's see. Today we've got sixteen kids to feed and Auntie Anne's over visiting too. Can't forget Mr. McCarty and myself. So that makes nineteen different orders. I'll go nice and slow, so you don't miss anything. Are you ready?"

I clutched my stomach so it wouldn't go berserk and did my best to tune out her long sing-song order. God knows how I didn't shove her aside. At last it was my turn. Mr. Ford peered over the counter at me. "Now what can I do for you, young Faul?"

My poor tongue almost tripped over itself. "Two serves of *chips*. Two serves of *fish*. Two battered *sausages*, please, sir." I passed him my money and ravenously watched my food being cooked and wrapped. Mr. Ford slid the precious newspaper parcel across the counter at me.

I ran outside and sank down on the nearest step so I could unwrap the paper and lift one big steaming, golden chip to my mouth. Pure perfection!

A dog approached, his eyes glued on the chip. My fingers froze mid-air as my heart sank to the pit of my stomach. "Oh no," I whispered in disbelief.

The dog plunked itself down right in front of me. It was a grubby, skinny mongrel, God only knew what parentage. Every one of his ribs was sticking out and his eyes stared at my chip with intense longing.

"No way!" I shouted. "Are you kidding? How does every one of you starving strays keep finding me?"

The dog ducked away at my voice but then helplessly returned and glued his melting eyes back on my food.

I had to get rid of him and quick before he started following me everywhere. I did not need another stray joining our gang. I was barely managing the six I had. I got to my feet and started backing away. The dog stared at me piteously. I waited until I was a bit of a distance away then quickly tossed two sausages at him. While the dog raced after them, I hugged my newspaper parcel of fish and chips to my chest and fled for my life back to the horse fair. I sat down on a stone to finish the rest in peace, my eyes swiveling everywhere while I tried cramming the lot down my gullet in record time. I had a sudden terrifying vision of me walking around Garryowen for the rest of my life with hundreds of starving dogs following me wherever I went. *How the hell was I going to say no to any more strays?*

I came to the last piece of battered fish. It was so beautifully cooked, but suddenly I couldn't eat any more. I couldn't get that poor starving dog out of my mind. *Heartless bastard,* I told myself in disgust. *That dog's exactly like you. Unwanted. Homeless. Looking for a bit of food and affection. Who are you to run away, saying you can't cope? Better go find the poor thing and make sure he's okay. Guess there's room for one more in the pack.* I retraced my steps, but the dog was gone. *One day, Martin,* I told myself, *you're going to want to leave Garryowen, and what's going to happen to your gang of dogs then? Who the hell's going to look after them?*

———

Things were heating up at the horse fair. Horses were selling fast. Chance Casey and the other horse brokers were run off their feet, fixing deal after deal. The really grand impressive stallions were now center stage, being ridden up and down a grassy space for all to see.

A horse took off, galloping like a lunatic to the end of the field. Men laughed and jeered and raised bottles of beer as it passed. The owner ran after it panicking. "Give you ten quid for the speedy two-legged donkey!" one wit yelled after him. The crowd laughed and raised their bottles again.

Chance was smoking his pipe, enjoying a well-earned break. Two young men wandered past him and lazily tossed their beer bottles and a crisp packet on the ground. Chance stepped quietly in front of them and lifted his eyes to meet theirs. "Ah, come on, fellas. Bit of respect for the place. This is an ancient burial mound. Our culture. We can't be tossing junk all over it."

I'd never heard Chance say so much.

Both men glared at him. One spat, narrowly missing Chance's boot. "Shut yer mouth, old man." He stuck his face in close, so they were eye to eye, noses touching. "Or this fist will take great pleasure in shutting it for ya."

They laughed and then elbowed rudely past.

Chance pulled his cap lower and stared down at the grass. I didn't want him knowing I'd witnessed his humiliation, so I slipped back in the crowd to see what he'd do next. I was curious to see how an outsider like me would handle these bullies. I have to admit he surprised me when he waited until the men were gone then quietly picked up the litter and gently put it in the trash. After that, he calmly re-lit his pipe and walked off.

Good for you, Chance. I thought.

He hadn't made a scene. He hadn't muttered anything bitter under his breath at the two oafs. He'd simply fixed the problem in his calm, quiet way, yet there'd been nothing cowardly about his actions.

It was like watching old Ireland meet new Ireland, and I sure knew which world I respected most.

⁓

Horse business done for the day, the crowd began moving over to the Fair Green Tavern. With nothing else to do, I wandered across with them.

It was a good opportunity to make some more money. I went straight up to the nearest man standing outside the door. "Hello, sir. Check on your horse in its trailer?"

The half-drunk farmer raised his pint of Guinness at me. "Good man. That's my grand fella in the blue horse truck over there."

I checked on the horse, ran back to give my report, and was flipped a coin. Soon I had enough money to buy myself a Coke and a packet of crisps. As soon as I started tearing open the packet with my teeth, a group of dogs appeared.

"Of course, you bloody lot would find me," I muttered. I shoved the crisps in my mouth while scanning the condition of the dogs. They all looked fit and well-fed. *Must belong to this horse crowd inside the pub.* "Sorry, fellas. If you're not a stray, then I'm not sharing."

Any dog that came over to annoy me for a pat or chip, I dealt with by turning my head away, closing my eyes, and crossing my arms.

The expressions on the dogs' faces were hilarious as if they were thinking, *Wowee, that human's actually talking dog at us! Can you believe it?*

When I stubbornly held the pose, they went to sniff each other instead. Some sat and discreetly watched me, intrigued.

I grinned. *Ha! That shut you up, didn't it?*

It didn't take long before I noticed a Jack Russell Terrier acting in a very unusual way. He was walking up to dogs much larger than himself. As he got closer, his little chin started straining upwards until his nose was pointing straight at the sky. His little stumpy tail went as high as it could too.

That's a bit weird, I thought, especially when the bigger dog started backing away, lowering its own nose.

Curious, I nicknamed the little dog "Shorty," and watched his progress as he went from dog to dog doing the same thing, even to an enormous Irish Wolfhound.

By now, I had gotten a feel for dog language. Any pose held unusually still by a dog meant something important was being said. Sure enough, the higher Shorty's chin went up, the lower the Irish Wolfhound's chin went down.

What Shorty was saying to each dog was clear: *I'm the boss around here, matey, not you. Show you agree by doing something subservient for me.*

To test my idea, I threw a crisp on the ground. Five dogs darted at it, but Shorty got in front and stopped. The rest stopped too. Stiff-legged, he walked past everyone until he was center stage. He raised his little chin straight up at the sky and held the pose for a long moment.

Instantly, all the other dogs lowered their chins, looked away, and backed off. Satisfied, Shorty walked over and daintily picked up the crisp, munching it happily. I grinned. Yep. Little Shorty sure was the undisputed boss of all these dogs, just as he had proclaimed.

Fascinated, I looked around to see if any other dogs were saying the same thing to each other, or was it only Shorty?

"Okay, my friends, what are your chins and tails saying to each other?" I asked quietly. It didn't take me long to realize how much dog politics was going on around me. It was like every dog in Garryowen was obsessed with same simple question: *Who's the leader of us two, and who's the follower?* Within seconds, each encounter ended with a decision. One dog would raise his chin and tail, clearly stating, *I'm boss.* The other would lower his chin and tail. *"Okay, you can be boss."* If neither dog gave in, there might be a bit of a scrap. Or perhaps a challenging test.

The quiet intensity and concentration of these encounters reminded me of Chance Casey and the farmers bargaining over a horse. Just like Chance, most of the hardest bargaining was done by silent, subtle signals, only instead of hands and fingers, the dogs used their whole bodies to negotiate.

I also noticed how often these strange dogs sniffed each other, and I remembered what Charlie Clarke had told me so many times, "A hoss can smell whether you're kind or sly, scared or brave, a leader or a follower. It's all in yer smell."

I hadn't really believed him before, but what if he was right? I already knew dogs smelled vital information about each other, from their health, their sex, to what they'd eaten—all that normal stuff. But what if these dogs were also trying to smell how confident the other dog felt? *Could dogs smell emotions?*

My eyes found Shorty again. He was sniffing a bulldog mongrel. It was a tense Mexican stand-off with neither dog showing signs of submission. Then the bulldog mongrel did something strange; he gave mixed signals. Low chin, high tail.

I suspected he was only faking submission. Shorty shared my suspicions. Narrowing his eyes like Clint Eastwood, he sniffed right under the tail of the faker. Clearly, something didn't smell right.

Fast as a snake, Shorty savaged the bulldog so he squealed and bolted, tail tucked right between his legs. The faker had been caught in a bare lie and punished.

Another idea hit me. Maybe that was why dogs tucked their tails up between their legs sometimes. To cover their bottoms so their true feelings couldn't be smelled by a competitor.

Pleased with himself, Shorty walked confidently around the clearing in front of the other dogs in a triumphant victory lap with his chin high, and his tail held up like a miniature banner. He was sending a clear message to each of the watching dogs: *Anyone else want to challenge me?* No dog dared. Satisfied, he sat in front of me. Impressed, I threw him another crisp. "No doubt about it, Shorty. You're game." He may have been small but he was ready to take on the world. It all came down to attitude.

From inside the pub, voices suddenly rose in anger. A glass banged down hard on a table. The crowd strained on tip-toe to see what was going on.

"You're *blind*, man! You were sold a mule. Just take a look at its *ears*, you fool. It's a mule you've bought yourself, for sure."

The owner of the disputed horse thumped the table again. "You shut up, Billy. What would you know?"

"Admit it, Pat. Yer were robbed. Yer always robbed if yer buy a hoss without my advice."

"Yeah? Come outside *now* and we'll sort out who's blind!" Two big men staggered out of the pub. The dogs and I scattered. The crowd followed happily, bringing out their drinks and lighting cigarettes. Some threw in some free advice.

"Mind yer watch his left fist, Pat. Got a devil of a kick in those knuckles of his, so I've heard."

Pat, meanwhile, was being held back by a friend. "Hold me back, Seamus! Hold me back, by God, before I burst his head!"

I shoved more crisps in my mouth and edged closer. Really, these men were no different than the dogs I had been watching. Every one needed to sort out who was dominant.

Without the calming influence of Chance Casey and the other horse brokers, it never took long for disputes to flare up—especially when the drink started to flow. The crowd cheered as a big hay-maker punch was thrown.

"You show him, Pat! Don't be shy!" someone shouted out, raising his glass.

I felt my stomach churning. The mood of the crowd was turning ugly. "Gotta get out of here," I muttered, feeling claustrophobic as the negative energy closed in on me.

I thought of little Shorty and how he'd used his subtle signals to keep peace among the dogs as he took control of the group. A thought hit me. These signals that both Shorty and Chance used were a form of polite language. *Were dogs more civilized than I thought?*

CHAPTER 9

Tige's Enchantment

I KNEW WELL THE IMPORTANCE OF CIVILIZED WORDS. THE day my brothers first called me stupid, everything changed between the three of us.

Dad had run out of money but desperately wanted a drink. He called the three of us to him and jerked a thumb towards the backyard. "Take the empty bottles from the shed down to the Pike Inn and get Ryan to swap them for Guinness. Should be enough to get me three full bottles."

It was a chance to impress Dad for once. We bolted for the shed like whippets.

"Don't piss about," yelled Dad after us. "Hurry straight there and back. I've had a hard day and I'm looking forward to a nice drink."

We staggered down to Pike Inn with armfuls of empties where Mr. Ryan reluctantly exchanged them for three full Guinness bottles. Geez, he could be a bitter old bugger. "There you go," he snapped. "Three full bottles." He eyed me unfavorably. "Mind you don't drink them yourselves."

My brothers looked at each other.

"We'll carry the bottles, Martin," said John. "You're sure to drop them."

117

Ha! I wasn't having any of that. "No way!" I snapped. "You two aren't stealing all the glory." Before they could stop me, I swept the bottles into my arms and marched off.

They tried wrestling the bottles from me, but I hung on for dear life until they gave up. Shrugging them off, I starting sprinting.

Andrew and John followed anxiously. "For God's sake, Martin, at least slow down."

"Geez, relax. Stop acting like a pair of nervous old grannies." The three of us were practically jogging now. Andrew and John hurried beside me, their eyes glued to the bottles in my arms.

"Dad will be so pleased," I said under my breath. "Nothing's going to go wrong. Here I am, Martin, the wonder son, helping out his dad." The happier I felt, the faster my feet sped up.

"Oh, God," said Andrew. "Wait, Martin!"

"I'm fine," I said over my shoulder. "Honestly, I feel great!"

I saw an unusual-looking mongrel up ahead. "Hi ya, little fella." I turned to get a better look and jogged backwards with the bottles cradled in my arms. The dog was a little beauty. Look at those markings. And those muscled little legs he had and . . .

"No!" screamed John and Andrew in unison.

My heel caught and sent me and the three bottles of Guinness flying. They smashed against the pavement. I hit the concrete and cracked my head loudly. All the air went out of me. *Ugh!* I opened my eyes to find the sky spinning around.

Andrew and John's faces glared down at me.

I couldn't believe what I'd done. I banged my head extra hard against the concrete to punish myself. "Why?" I yelled and banged my head harder. "Why do I always screw things up?"

John was moaning in horror. "Oh, my God. Oh, my God. We're going to die."

"I didn't drop them," muttered Andrew, panicking. "Why's he going to kill me?" He looked at the mess and kicked me hard in the thigh. "What am I saying? Of course, he's going to kill me! All because I let you carry his precious fucking bottles of Guinness! Why are you so stupid, Martin?"

"Everyone's right," yelled John. "You *are* incredibly stupid!"

"Stop calling me stupid!" I roared, leaping to my feet. The three of us faced each other, ready to fight.

Of all the things they'd ever said to me, my brothers had never called me stupid before. It was the one sacred thing they never said. Now the ugly word hung in the air between us. Side by side, they glared at me, their arms folded, their faces stony.

I stared back, shocked. It was like they were throwing me out of our gang of three. I suddenly felt queasy. Deep down they must think I really was a moron like everyone said. Their belief in my intelligence had always helped me shut out all the cruel taunts ever since I could remember.

Maybe I *was* a moron. I ran off and stayed away from home until it started raining. Dad was waiting for me with his belt.

"I was really looking forward to that Guinness," he growled.

"Sorry," I said numbly. The belting hurt but I lived. What hurt more was that one word John and Andrew had finally thrown in my face. *Stupid.* I think that was the day I started to drift apart from them, the day I decided I could survive without them.

That night I slept in the coal shed again. Dad had *really* wanted those three Guinnesses. As I curled up with Major and Rex, the thought crossed my mind that not only did dogs calm me down, they never made me feel stupid.

One man in Garryowen who never made me feel stupid was Tige Kelly. To me he was like Merlin from the legends of King Arthur.

He was the old headmaster of St. Patrick's School, a friend of Mammy's, and our godfather. He'd been dead a few years but I still couldn't forget him. While he was alive, the teachers didn't shout at me so much. He'd been my protector and mentor.

He'd been a striking man. Tall and straight-backed. Hair swept back in sleek, silver waves. Eyes that were kind and piercing. When I was older and heard David Attenborough speaking on TV, I thought, "Wow. He has Tige Kelly's voice."

He lived in a big, Edwardian house with his brother and sister, surrounded by beautiful furniture. The chairs were covered in fine silk. On the table there was always a beautiful tray with the tallest, fanciest cake. There were delicate china cups Mammy knew how to use while we three boys had plastic cups full of lemonade.

Even better than those lovely cakes, Tige Kelly's house was where my brain finally had a chance to feast on fine conversation. My ADHD went to sleep whenever we went there.

I listened as he and Mammy discussed Europe and politics, history, and art.

"How do you know so much, Mammy?" I asked in awe one day. I'd never heard her talk like this at home.

"Books," she laughed.

Great, no chance of me learning any of it then.

"Even if you can't read yet, school can be a place where you start a life-long love affair with learning," Tige said, turning to me with a smile.

"Geez. Good luck with *that*," I said darkly.

He smiled and cut me a large slice of cake. "No matter what happens at school, Martin, try to learn something new every day for the rest of your life," he said. "Only a fool thinks he knows everything."

I didn't know anything. "I'll try," I promised.

"Have you heard of a boy called Setanta?" Tige asked me on one visit.

"No. Does he live on the Garryowen estate?"

"No, but he did live a long time ago," he said, "in the legends of ancient Ireland." He paused to let me settle in. "Setanta was no ordinary boy," he continued. "He was destined to be the most famous warrior in all Ireland. Even as a young boy he earned himself a great warrior name—Cuchulainn—pronounced *Coo-cull-in*." He smiled. "This is the strange way he earned his famous name." I felt myself slipping effortlessly under Tige's enchantment.

"Once," he said, "long ago, there was an Irish boy called Setanta. As soon as he was old enough, he went to live with King Conchobor. This was the King of Ulster and a very wealthy man. One day the king decided to visit his special blacksmith named Culann and share a big feast with him. He invited the boy Setanta to come with him.

'I'll come along later,' said Setanta. 'I want to practice with my hurling stick a bit longer.'

The king arrived at the blacksmith's, but forgot Setanta was following behind him.

'Is anyone coming after you?' asked the blacksmith.

'No,' said the king.

'Then I'll shut my gates and release my great hound to guard us,' said the blacksmith. 'But beware! My savage hound is so ferocious that three chains are needed to hold him. In fact, he's so strong, it takes three strong men hanging on to each chain to hold him back.'

'Hmmm, that *is* impressive,' said the king.

'Living in such a wild place, I need him to guard my home and cattle from my enemies,' the blacksmith explained. He gestured at his men. 'Shut the gates, but beware. If anyone's unlucky to be left outside, they'll surely be ripped to shreds by my dog.' So the gates were shut and the great savage hound was released.

Not long after, the boy Setanta arrived at the blacksmith's home. He was having fun casually tapping his ball up in the air with his hurley stick as he walked along, seeing how long he could keep it airborne. The huge hound saw him and ran straight for the boy to rip him apart. But Setanta was brave and a quick thinker. He didn't panic. Instead, he tossed aside his hurley stick and ball so he could tackle the hound with his bare hands. He grabbed its throat with one hand, its back with the other and raised it up high and smashed it hard against the nearest log pillar. He threw it so hard, the dog's limbs fell from their sockets. The dog was dead before it hit the ground.

Hearing all the commotion, the gates were quickly unbarred and everyone rushed outside to see what had happened.

Culann, the blacksmith, stared at his dead dog lying in the dirt in horror. 'What have you done, boy?' he said. 'My household will be like a desert with the loss of such a wonderful hound! He was so loyal he guarded my life, my honor, my home and my cattle. He was a valued servant and now you've taken him from me.'

Setanta thought for a moment. 'Don't worry. I know how to fix this. I'll rear a pup from the same pack for you. While it grows, I'll be your hound and do its job. I'll guard your home and cattle for you. When it's big enough I'll leave, and your new dog can continue to guard you well.'

It was a wise idea.

The king's druid turned to Setanta and said importantly for all to hear, 'Know this as a great moment. From now on, this boy Setanta shall be known as *Cuchulainn*. It means the *Hound of Culann* and one day, boy, you'll be the most famous warrior in all Ireland.'"

I sat back, fascinated. Finally, a kid who impressed me.

"The druid was right," said Tige Kelly. "For Cuchulainn is still Ireland's most legendary hero today."

I looked at Tige and felt a surge of excitement. "Geez. I'm just like Cuchulainn, aren't I? I'm brave and good at hurling. I bet I could have protected myself against that blacksmith's guard dog too."

He smiled. "Yes, if you lived thousands of years ago, I believe you would have become a great warrior in ancient Ireland just like Cuchulainn."

It was like a door had been thrown open for me. There was finally a place I might have belonged where I wouldn't have felt like a useless, unwanted freak. Pity I couldn't travel back in time.

Tige was passionate about saving Ireland's ancient culture. He was adamant I should never forget the importance of passing on the old Irish legends to future generations. "Each story from our Irish past," he said, "is a gift you must pass on to others." His mesmerizing eyes drew me in. "On your last day on earth will you be proud of how much you helped pass on your culture to others? Or will you realize too late you played a part in losing Ireland's old precious stories forever?"

After a visit with Tige, I'd be so enthralled by all the old Irish legends, I'd start imagining myself as a great Celtic warrior heading out on a raid to steal cattle. Here I was riding my horse past standing stones through herds of valuable cattle. Galloping past grave mounds of great kings. Finding my way through vast oak forests that spread from coast to coast. Seeing legendary Irish kings and warriors in their battle chariots. Hearing their rousing speeches before leading their fierce armies into famous battles.

I was running through a great, mythical land where magic, honor, courage, and action ruled supreme.

Suddenly, I tripped and crashed to earth, my imagination coming to a screeching halt. All I could see was Garryowen Estate spreading in all directions.

Boring, boring Garryowen.

Instead of a wild, proud Ireland, all I could see was suburbia. Tidy roads lined with little boxes of identical houses. Far too many brick walls, pavement, and gutters dividing everything into little concrete territories. Everywhere there were ordinary people doing ordinary things.

My ears caught bits of conversations as I walked past houses as fast as I could.

"Jim! Come in now and fix the washing machine! I still can't get the nuisance of a thing to work."

"Hi, Maureen. Do us a favor? Mind the little ones while I dash up to the shops and get some fags."

I sped up, trying to escape. Down that street was the bloody hateful St. Patrick's School, the place that tried its best to crush every spark of spirit out of me. Worse, right across the road from our house was that dour statue of St. Patrick. "You can buzz off too," I yelled, and meant it. I hated the guy. His name was stamped over Garryowen so much it sometimes felt like we were stuck living deep inside the St. Patrick Empire.

I went to St. Patrick's School, played for the St. Patrick's hurling team, lived across the road from St. Patrick's Well, which was an ancient pagan sacred well that now belonged to *him*. Nearby was an ancient stone sticking out of the grass that had been named "St. Patrick's Donkey" after the poor animal supposedly died there and was transformed into a rock. You couldn't escape the guy.

It was funny being surrounded by his empire when he had been an escaped slave himself. He'd dragged Christianity to my country, and used it to bring the whole proud Celtic warrior culture crashing down. As far as I could see, he'd made our proud nation of Irish people feel guilt, shame, and helplessness like never before.

I stared at all that dreary suburbia threatening to suffocate me. My frustration was boiling until it felt like the top of my head was about to burst open like Cuchulainn's when he went into a legendary war-spasm. *Why the hell was I stuck living in Garryowen now? I should have been born two thousand years ago!* It was crazy. Back in ancient times, no one would have despised my hyperactivity. Not at all. In fact, they would have admired it. Nor would anyone have cared about my not being able to read or write. Actually, I reckoned, the ancient Celts would have *loved* me.

And why not? As a triplet, I would have been considered magical. The number three was seen to possess great magic by the superstitious Celts, and back then triplets were rare. In the Gaelic Games Association we'd been told we were the first triplet boys in recorded history to play hurling.

I knew the Celts might have been cruel sometimes, but I still preferred their fierce, passionate culture to the watered down, boring Christian Ireland I saw around me. The Celts had celebrated Irish people who stood proud, having honor, courage, a witty tongue, and intelligence. Everything I admired.

My feet started running again, taking me out into the fields and countryside. At least out here I could pretend I was living in ancient times.

"Martin, someone cursed you to be born in the wrong year," I panted under my breath. It was a punishment so awful I wouldn't have wished it on my worst enemy.

CHAPTER 10

Supreme Boss of All the Dogs

I HAD FELT DEEPLY TROUBLED AFTER MY DAY AT THE Garryowen Horse Fair.

I couldn't stop thinking of Shorty, the Jack Russell terrier. He'd been the supreme boss of all the dogs at the pub. Did that mean there was a supreme boss of our gang too?

There was no way I wanted the seven of us bickering endlessly over who was in charge. I'd run away from home to escape that kind of hell.

"Of course we're okay. We're the Dirty Dog Gang," I said aloud like a mantra. We were all equals, the very best of friends, weren't we?

The dogs were waiting for me in the loft in Padraig's barn when I returned from stealing my breakfast, and erupted out of the hay to greet me.

"Whoa!" I said, stepping backwards.

They threw themselves all over me, jumping up to lick me. No wonder I never felt lonely. How could I when they always smothered me with such affection?

"What have you lazy dogs been up to, huh?" I reached down to pat them and pull stalks of hay from their fur. "Have a nice nap?"

They kept leaping up on me, even rougher than before.

"Relax, you idiots, or you'll hurt me."

Mossy jumped so high, he managed to drag his tongue right across my mouth. "*Ugh!* Do you mind?" Disgusted, I rubbed his saliva off my lips. Red scratched my leg with his claws. Pa barged against me so hard, I almost lost my footing. Missy was yapping her head off, chasing her tail in circles. Fergus was bouncing around like a wiry Ping-Pong ball.

Yeah, everyone was acting normally.

Exhausted, I flopped back in the hay, letting the dogs swarm all over me. That's when I saw something that made me freeze. *You're kidding!* I pushed Mossy and Fergus off.

It was Missy. She was trying to jump up and lick Red on the face in the same manic way she'd leapt up on me, only he hated it. He tilted his chin up as high as it could go and growled, showing his gums.

I knew that raised chin signal. It was the same signal Shorty had used so much. It was the one that said, *I'm the boss of us two.*

Missy ignored it and kept leaping up to lick his face rudely. He growled in warning, more threatening than before. When she still didn't stop, he attacked her until she squealed and rolled over to expose her belly.

My stomach dipped. It was just as I feared. The dogs weren't greeting me with affection! All that jumping and licking and clawing was their way of competing with each other to see who could dominate me the most. The bastards! I could see their game now.

Whoever dominates stupid Martin the most gets to be boss of the gang.

My mind was whirling as everything fell into place. I'd assumed the dogs were swarming over me because they liked me so much. Instead, they'd seen me as the weakest member of our gang. Every day they'd been proving how submissive I was by invading my body—my personal space—any way they could.

I was so angry that I looked around for something to throw at them, but nothing was in reach except stupid clumps of hay, which I snatched up in handfuls and threw as hard as I could.

They just stood there, grinning at me, hay tumbling harmlessly off their faces and backs. "I can't believe you've all been treating me like such an idiot! The real dumbo of our gang!" I yelled.

Pa scratched a flea, obviously bored.

"None of you act like that towards each other—only me! That's how *pathetic* you think I am! How *dare* you treat me with so little respect after everything I've done for you!" I had never felt so betrayed. I rubbed away tears angrily. "I *trusted* you dogs!" I shouted, thumping the hay. "More than anyone else— even my own brothers. All along you've been secretly throwing my friendship back in my face!"

I went to get up, but the dogs rushed at me again, nearly knocking me off my feet. All of them were shoving and pushing each other aside, trying to stand on my stomach as they frantically blocked my way. Trapped, I slapped them away from licking my face.

Their claws really hurt. Their tongues were disgusting! They were clearly dominating me. It was just like when Andrew and John held me down to tickle me to prove they were stronger and that I was just the runt triplet.

"Get lost!" I hollered as I shoved the dogs off me. By now I was trembling with rage. "So much for being part of a gang among fucking friends! Hope you feel ashamed of yourselves!"

They didn't look the slightest bit sorry. Most of them started scratching lazily or sniffing each other. They didn't even bother moving. Pa scratched under his chin, glancing at me in a bored way. *Yeah, yeah, kid, have another silly temper tantrum. Who cares?*

I had to get away from them. As I started for the ladder I realized Mossy was following me. I whipped around and pointed a furious finger straight at him. "As for you! I always thought you were my *best* friend! Instead you were dominating me the most! What a snake in the grass you turned out to be!"

I needed to get away from these traitors. I ran straight out into the rain not caring if Padraig saw me. So much for having dogs as friends. Now I hated them, too.

<hr />

Of course, I came back that afternoon. I had nowhere else to go and I was drenched and shivering. I had never felt lonelier in my life, but, even so, I wanted to see the dogs again. Maybe I'd been wrong about them.

The moment I climbed up the ladder, the dogs ran straight at me like a furry tidal wave. "Bugger off!" I thundered at them.

They fell back in surprise.

"I know all your little tricks now," I snapped.

Mossy, however, wasn't giving up easily. He leapt up and managed to lick me across the mouth. The next time he tried it, I kneed him in the chest and he fell back in the hay. All the dogs were watching me warily now.

"So, my friends," I said sarcastically. "Here's how it's going to be from now on. If there has to be a boss of this gang, then that boss is going to be *me*."

Mossy made another run at me but I kneed him again and raised my chin very high in the air as I had seen Shorty do.

My body language conveyed, *I'm the boss now, and I mean it.* I crossed my arms for emphasis. *And I mean it!* I might have been the runt of my brothers, the least important member of my family, and the dunce of my school, but there was no way I was letting six stray street dogs put one over on me.

One by one the dogs lowered their noses and took their seats around me. A few lay down looking very submissive and apologetic.

I started breathing easier. "Don't blame me. I wanted us all to be friends. You dogs are the ones who've turned our gang upside down like this." I wasn't happy, of course, but the alternative was to move out and live on my own. Ha! I knew *that* wasn't going to happen. Without the dogs, I'd die of boredom and loneliness within a week. "I'm no loser," I said, "so everyone better stop treating me like one."

I spent an hour making sure they understood I was the new leader of our gang. How? I kept calling them to me and kneeing anyone who jumped up. I stood on my tip-toes until they stopped swarming over me in manic excitement and finally treated me with polite respect instead.

I flopped back in the hay, exhausted, and growled so they wouldn't come and jump on me. They kept staring at me uncertainly, upon which I turned my head away and yawned. *Go away and relax. It's all sorted out now. I'm in charge.*

The dogs shook themselves in relief and wandered off, sat down and started licking themselves. I felt the tension leave the room instantly. That little lesson in manners had been exhausting but worth it. "I'm never letting you lot swarm all over me ever again," I said firmly. "So be warned."

It was hard not to take their behavior personally, but I couldn't help thinking that maybe I was being too harsh with them. Then I remembered how they always tried to dominate *everyone* with their manic energy and affection—not just me. How many hours had I watched them endlessly try to one up each other as well as other dogs or any cats or horses they came across?

They couldn't help themselves. I understood that now. All that manic behavior wasn't personal. It was just them being dogs.

I called a truce before bedtime. "Dogs, I forgive you, but be warned. You won't be dominating me in that old way ever again." To be honest, I was secretly nervous. If I was their leader, was everything going to change? Would this mean the end of our gang? Over the next few months, I studied the dogs carefully and was shocked to learn they tried to dominate each other almost all the time.

I scratched my head. "Jesus! How the hell didn't I notice what was going on before? You dogs just don't ever stop competing against each other, do you?" I found most of their dominating was done by means of a secret, playful game. At first I had no idea how to play it, or what the rules were, but after a while, I came to know it very well and played it myself.

This secret game changed how I talked to dogs forever.

These months were a very exciting time of discovery for me. The weather was terribly wet and usually this would have driven me demented with boredom. This time, it was different. The hay barn became our private classroom, and the dogs my teachers.

I learned that the dogs woke up every morning and started testing each other right away to see who the boss of the gang should be that day. They were also trying to work out everyone's pecking order.

The dogs did this by tossing little challenges at each other. For example, Red might step on Missy's toes, so Red was the winner. Or Pa might grab an old bone from Fergus and walk around the loft, showing it off like a victory trophy. Fergus might race to the top of the hay stack and beat all the other dogs, so he won the race challenge.

Just like humans, the dogs reacted differently to each challenge. Fergus always looked jaunty when he won. Blackie was always surly, whether he won *or* lost. Missy looked a little sly when she tried to win a challenge and quickly lost her temper when she lost too often. Pa was happy when he won, and took a nap when he lost too much. Red was a noble winner and just as noble at losing. Mossy was the real surprise. He was *extremely* competitive and desperately strived to win every single challenge against me. It was obvious we both wanted to be the leader of the gang.

"I'll beat you," I said confidently. "There's no way a little spaniel's going to be *my* boss!" He grinned back. I quite think he liked the new me and was glad I'd finally started playing the game. We were definitely the top two rivals in this secret game of dogs.

After a few days, I noticed some challenges were more important than others, so I mentally started awarding points to each one. Just like in any human game, the dogs were trying to score more points than each other.

Most of the gang stepped on each other's toes when they thought they could get away with it, so I awarded that easy challenge only one point per win. Only Mossy and Blackie took this challenge seriously. They growled at any dog who dared to stand on *their* toes. Red was clever at winning this challenge. He kept clumsily backing into other dogs, so he "accidentally" ended up treading on their toes. Blackie always bit him if he tried this trick.

A challenge worth a lot more points was when one dog jumped up on another dog and rested his paws on the other dog's shoulders. It always caused a strong reaction, sometimes even a fight, so I gave this challenge a value of ten points. Mossy was constantly doing this and he won lots of points this way.

Other ways of invading someone's personal space could score you points. You could do this by using your claws, body, or even your tongue to get through another dog's defenses. It didn't matter whether a dog was small and friendly like Missy or big and aggressive like Blackie; they each had plenty of ways of winning points against the rest of us.

Missy had a clever trick. She'd pretend to spin around chasing her tail. Then she'd crash into another dog and playfully lick and claw his face in the confusion. It was a great way of winning four or five points in a few seconds before darting out of reach.

Pa liked leaning against other dogs, especially when he chewed at a pretend flea at the base of his tail. Each time he leaned in, he earned a few points.

Of course, all the dogs constantly tried to win points against me. I was the prime target and invading my personal space was definitely their favorite way of scoring points. Missy was very good at it. She had a habit of testing my balance by weaving around my feet until I tripped. If she did manage to trip me, she won a point. However, if she could get me to trip and fall to the ground, then I reckoned that was worth about thirty points. She also liked to lick me all over my hands and arms. Each lick was worth half a point at least. Mossy's licks were different. He went for the surprise attack. Suddenly he'd bounce up and slip his tongue straight inside my mouth. To him, my lips were like goal posts scoring him maybe twenty points or so. He was shoving his scent right into me where I couldn't ignore it. All the dogs loved trying to jump up on me, especially when I returned to the barn. I soon realized they were trying to plant their scent on my body. This scent came from the undersides of their paws. It was like leaving an invisible victory mark on your competitor. The higher a dog planted its smell on me, the more points it won.

Each dog had a few specialties. They practiced these until they were brilliant at winning, and I soon found myself admiring the dogs for their ingenuity. Pa had a simple trick that won him lots of points from everyone. He'd pretend to be so lazy he couldn't get up if you needed to walk past. It was funny how he always picked strategic places to lie across, like doorways and the top of the wall ladder. By deliberately lying in the way, he forced the other dogs to jump awkwardly over him or make an annoying detour. This may have won him only one or two points at a time, but these easy points soon added up. I could trust Pa to work out the laziest possible way to win points. Pa's more active approach was to barge others out of his way. The more he knocked someone off his feet, the more points he won. A gentle bump against my leg might be worth one point, while knocking me completely off my feet was worth at least thirty points for him.

Fergus's method, on the other hand, was just as ingenious. If another dog had a sleeping spot he wanted, he'd pretend there was an intruder outside and would run to the edge of the loft, barking at the imaginary enemy. Then he'd start racing back and forth barking as if to say, *There's someone out there! An intruder! Let's go scare it away together!* All the dogs would rush past him and slide down the haystack to see what was going on outside. As soon as they left, Fergus would stroll past me nonchalantly. Within seconds, he'd be curled up in the most comfy sleeping hole in the hay, then promptly fall asleep. The rest of the dogs would troop wearily back up the hay stack, dripping wet from the rain and irritated at having their time wasted. Disgusted, they'd look at Fergus dozing, then sit down to begin the long, boring process of licking themselves dry. It was a clever ploy that always worked and won Fergus about twenty or thirty points each time. Fergus also taught me that *nudging* for attention was another way to win. I thought all he was doing was shoving at my hand for a pat until I realized each nudge was worth half a point. He could quickly score a lot of points pretending to be affectionate, especially when I was distracted or sleepy.

Mossy had a favorite ploy that had me baffled for months. He'd wake up in the morning, shake off any hay and wander *almost* all the way over to me. He'd be about five feet away, acting as though his feet were suddenly cemented to the hay. Patiently, he'd stand there, his tail wagging slowly, his head a fraction lower than usual, and his big spaniel eyes looking at me in a heart-melting way.

"Silly dog," I'd laugh as I walked over to give him his morning pat. "Why don't you come all the way to me? Bit lazy, aren't you?" After a while, however, I became suspicious and realized he was trying to lure *me* into walking over to him. I finally worked out how the challenge worked: It was a basic contest of wills. With each step he tricked me into taking towards him, the more important he felt. Cheeky bugger! "Damn!" I laughed, looking around at the dogs. "You've all been tricking me with that one haven't you?"

Then there were the simple races of who could get to the top of the haystack first, or who could run to greet someone first, or who slid down the stack first. There were so many challenges! Some that proved you were faster or braver or smarter or stronger or more adaptable than anyone else. Basically, all were designed to prove one thing: who was best qualified to lead the pack.

Sometimes I felt more like a dog than a human. I certainly preferred the simplicity of the dog world. For dogs, life was easy. If you won more points than another dog, then you were more important than he was. For once I knew exactly what was expected of me. In this world I was a highly respected champion, not a loser.

After a month I looked at Mossy. "Reckon I'm nearly the undisputed leader of this gang now," I said confidently.

But I would soon find out that he still had a few tricks up his sleeve.

—◦—

I learned to question *everything* I knew about dogs. Even something as simple as *where* you touched a dog had important political meaning in the dog world. If I touched a dog under its chin and on the chest, I was actually telling it, *Hi dog, let me be more submissive than you.* His chin and tail would rise higher as his attitude became more challenging. He'd puff out his chest proudly. *Yeah, Martin, keep patting me there. I'm winning a point every time you touch me, so keep on going. Give me more free points. More! More!"*

I soon learned to rub, not pat, the dogs on top of their heads, necks, shoulders, and backs. That was my way of saying, *Relax, dog. I'm more dominant than you, so no need to challenge me.*

Funny enough, I found the dogs kept perfect score in this game of winning points, perhaps because their whole lives revolved around playing it. Even I became good at keeping separate scores against each dog. The more I did it, the easier it became. Everyone knew who was winning and who was losing, who was having an off day or a particularly victorious day.

It wasn't long before I found myself getting sucked into playing the game all the time until I was just as obsessed as the dogs were. "No cheating, Pa," I'd laugh. "You don't get to eat until after Blackie. He's won much more points than you lately." Blackie would then gratefully accept his food from my fingers. He was much more polite now that I knew how the game was played. He didn't try to snatch food from me and hardly growled at all. I now understood why Blackie hated dogs running past him. It was too tempting an opportunity for them to veer close and try to bump him. So he developed zero tolerance to it. All dogs walked *very* politely past Blackie or got attacked. I took his advice and didn't let the dogs rush past me either. Now they couldn't barge against my legs and knock me off balance.

Seeing how wonderfully behaved the dogs were now, I put even more effort into understanding how the secret dog game was played. It was worth it to see them so happy, and it was beneficial to me as well.

They respected me inside the barn and out on walks. They came straight to me when I called them. They shut up immediately when I asked them to stop barking. They stopped endlessly bickering with each other. Almost all their violent fights stopped. They didn't keep annoying me when I was trying to relax.

They became so well-behaved that our barn was a haven of peace. Most of the time I *loved* playing this secret game because it made my life so much easier. I had learned that the secret to having a well-behaved dog was winning enough points to be its undisputed leader.

If I messed up their simple points system, I soon brought total chaos down upon us all. Horrible dog fights broke out. They rudely ran off and ignored me when I called them. They started chasing the farmer's cows and chickens. They barked too much and wouldn't shut up. They basically drove me crazy.

One night when I was feeling particularly lonely, I insisted on us having no pecking order. Equality for all! But this idea failed spectacularly when everything exploded into the most vicious dog fight yet.

My stomach churned as I tried to break them up fast as I could. Afterwards, I sank down into the hay, a nervous wreck, my heart racing. I knew the stupid fight was my fault and that the dogs were bleeding because of my stubbornness. After that failed experiment, I played the secret game more diligently than ever and the fights came to an end.

The pecking order in our pack never really changed. I was the leader. Mossy was top dog. Then Blackie, Red, Pa, and Missy. And poor Fergus was always last. I felt sorry for him and tried to make him more important than grumpy Blackie and lazy Pa, but they kept attacking him so I stopped. I finally accepted that it wasn't up to me to change their order of dominance. Their own personalities made that decision.

Stop interfering, Martin, I'd tell myself firmly. *This strict pecking order is the way the dogs keep themselves civilized. It's their way of keeping the peace.* I was learning that the dog world had even *more* rules than the human world and they were strictly enforced. No dog could ever be equal to another and the punishment for breaking this important rule was to be viciously attacked.

No wonder the dogs had been growling at me every now and then since I'd met them. I'd been breaking every rule in their world! "Geez, sorry about that," I said into the darkness after blowing the candle out one night. "You've all been patient with me. I appreciate it."

After a few months something had profoundly changed between the seven of us. I knew what it meant: The dogs had finally made me the leader of the gang. Instead of feeling boastful, I actually felt humbled. My friends had decided they trusted me to take charge. They were ready to follow whatever decision I made without hesitation. I may not have been a success among humans, but in the dog world I was a supreme champion. I only hoped I was worthy of the gang's trust.

CHAPTER 11

Fight Back or Give In Forever

I STILL REMEMBER THE MOMENT THAT I FINALLY FOUND THE courage to stand up to my father. It was one of the most frightening things I'd ever done in my life, but I knew that it was time to stop his bullying. I took my stand over my haircut.

"You look like a bloody girl," he had snapped at me one day right in front of my brothers. "You're not leaving the house until that ridiculous mane comes off." He had his own ideas about how short a healthy young Irish male should keep his hair. Regulation army style. No more than half an inch of stubble. Andrew and John couldn't be bothered arguing with him, so kept their hair short without any drama.

Of course, I rebelled. "Keeping my hair just the way it is," I said sullenly. *God, why can't he just leave me alone?* For some reason I always equated hair with freedom. God knows why. Maybe because of the Rolling Stones and other rock bands. I was also embarrassed by my ears that stuck out like door knobs.

"Fetch the scissors and my razor," he ordered Andrew. He kicked a chair forward and gestured impatiently for me to sit.

"No, you're not turning me into some shaved weirdo," I said fiercely, standing my ground. "You'll have to tie me down before you give me another one of your stupid haircuts."

My dad couldn't believe his ears. He stuck a finger in one, wriggled it around as though cleaning it out. "What did you say?"

"You heard me alright, you big bully. I'm keeping this hair. It's mine." I'd never been so cheeky to him.

"Sit down this *instant*, boy, before I flay you alive!"

I bolted out the front door before he could catch me. The scissors banged off the door lintel above me, and I ducked. "Missed, you old fool!" I yelled over my shoulder as I kept running and laughing.

When he wanted to, my father could be a very patient man. He hid himself behind the kitchen door, and when I came back two hours later, he grabbed my arm, put a knee in my back and started hacking at my hair.

It was now or never. I had to fight back or give in forever, so I grabbed a saucepan lying on the table and cracked him over the skull. His expression was so dumbfounded it might have been comical if I wasn't so angry—or so scared. "I'm not a bloody dog you can bully around!" I screamed. "You think you're some big tough man, but really you're a stupid old loser who drinks too much. Believe me, you'd think twice about holding me down and giving me a haircut if I was the same size as you." I'd never stood up to him so brazenly before, but I knew if I didn't start fighting back hard, he was on the point of crushing my spirit forever.

He was so stunned that his mouth opened and closed like a goldfish with no words coming out.

After that, things only got worse. My dad really couldn't bear how I was standing up to him more. His drinking increased and he became more violent. Despite the danger, I couldn't stop speaking back cheekily at him whether he was drunk or sober.

"Yeah? You're thinking twice about hitting me now, aren't you? Not so easy to belt me now I'm not cowering in a corner."

And then there was the endless war I was fighting at school with the St. Pat teachers—especially Mr. Keeley and Mr. Rollins—who enjoyed having me as their whipping boy. Often it seemed as if I was getting belted every single day at school. My body was constantly covered with bruises.

My new rebellious mood followed me to class every day where I heard Mr. Keeley's voice dripping with sarcasm.

"Faul! Stop staring out the window like a moronic idiot. Sit down this instant!" By this point I knew how to get my revenge on Keeley, which was to make the class laugh along with me instead of him.

"Sure I'll sit—when you stop boring the bollocks off me."

My classmates tittered happily. I already knew what he'd do next.

"Go straight to the headmaster's office and wait for him!" he bellowed.

Excellent! Just what I wanted him to say. I was in for a filthy caning of course, but at least I could escape the torture of listening to Keeley's droning voice. And it was time for a feed anyway.

Slouching out the door, I made a straight line to the lunch bags hanging along the hall wall. As I started rifling through them, I decided which lunches looked the nicest. "Mmm. Chocolate cake. Egg sandwiches. Biscuits. A jam scone. Peanut butter on a biscuit—that'll do nicely." I busily helped myself like it was a self-serve cafeteria. "Ooh, thank you, Pat. Your mam always packs such lovely ham and cheese sandwiches. Very fancy." I cradled the lunches in my arms as I wolfed them down while slowly heading to the headmaster's office.

I finally reached the headmaster's office door and found it open. Our old headmaster Tige Kelly had died of a heart attack (which devastated me), and we had a new one—Mr. Crowe. He didn't understand or protect me the way Tige had. I peered cautiously inside. His office was empty. *La-la-la!*

My eyes flickered everywhere as I idly wondered where Mr. Crowe kept his lunch then they fell upon his briefcase and nearly popped out of my head. The man had left it unlocked. Was he an idiot?

My ten thieving fingers went wild undoing the strap. I opened the case wide and peered in. *Aaaaaah!* The brief case was loaded with treasure!

It was filled to the brim with little cardboard collection boxes full of coins. It was part of the Pope's campaign to save starving children affected by the famines raging through Africa. The teachers had handed out these little boxes and instructed us to fill them with loose change. Photos of little African children stared up at me. My trembling fingers picked up one of the glorious little beauties. It was so heavy, it was like holding a bar of gold and clinked every time I tilted it.

Decision time. I could put the box back into the briefcase, pull the strap closed, and stand in the corner, or . . . ?

My fingers had no shame and before I could blink, they took over completely. All of a sudden I was wriggling out of my sweater and throwing it across the desk. I dumped the cardboard boxes on it, wrapped the sweater into a ball, and, hugging it to my chest, I dashed outside the building.

"Treat me worse than a dog?" I muttered. "Well, here's what you get—a real animal of a kid who doesn't give a shit." I galloped to the farm next door, hoping no one saw me.

Headmaster Crowe was guaranteed to go completely psycho because he'd have to explain to the parish priest why the boxes of money had gone missing while in his care. But where the hell was I going to hide them? No place at home. Besides, that'd be the first place they'd look. My eyes drifted over the rock wall in front of me. Who'd think of looking for the money out here in the middle of a field?

"Try finding them here, Mr. 'Clever' Crowe," I said, pulling some rocks out of the wall and stashing the boxes inside the natural cavity.

Grinning, I leaned forward and kissed the hiding place. My stash was safe. Even better, I'd finally had my revenge on that hated school. "Well, teachers, do your worst. I'll *never* tell you where I've hidden the money."

I took a deep breath and walked back to the headmaster's office, my head held high, a defiant glint in my eye. I knew what was coming but didn't care.

The teachers were enraged. But whenever they screamed, "Where's the Pope's money?!" I just looked at them blankly.

The beatings that followed were terrible. I was threatened with Hell and eternal damnation, and even an interview with the Pope himself. The Gardaí were called. But there was nothing they could do because there was no evidence to prove I took the money.

That was my real revenge on the teachers: showing them that all the physical violence in the world wouldn't beat me.

—⌣—

My brothers tried to talk me into giving up. "You better tell them where you hid the money," said John, "or those teachers are going to make your life hell." We were lying on our bed up in our bedroom talking.

I shrugged. "I'm not scared of the teachers."

Andrew shook his head. "Dad'll flog it out of you sooner or later," he warned.

"I'm not afraid of Dad either." But then I heard the sound of his boots on the stairs. "Quick!" I said. "Let's escape out the window."

"We haven't done anything wrong," said Andrew sulkily. "Why should we go anywhere?"

"Fine. Stay," I snapped. "You can both continue the discussion with his belt on your own."

Cursing me, they followed me out the window and down the drain pipe, ducking around the side of the house while Dad's yelling exploded upstairs.

"Let's take Major and Rex with us," I suggested.

"Okay, I'll slip out the back and get the leashes from the shed," offered John.

"I'll get the dogs from the backyard," said Andrew. I felt relieved the dogs were coming. Although I was no longer afraid of my father or the teachers, there were men in Garryowen who genuinely scared me. Hard men, bad men like those from the O'Brien Clan.

My brothers and I met the O'Brien's that afternoon for the first time. As we walked Major and Rex across the fields, we found ourselves in a small stand of trees. "What the hell's that?" asked Andrew, hearing a strange noise.

We listened hard. Major and Rex started whining and pulling on their leashes, eager to be released.

"Sounds like dogs fighting," said John. "Quick! We'd better break them up!"

We started running towards the noise, and Major and Rex were hauling so hard on their leashes, they nearly pulled John and Andrew over. We broke through the trees and came upon something much worse than a dog fight. It took a while for me to understand what was happening.

Badger baiting.

There were three men—one older, two younger—standing around a pile of freshly dug dirt. It was a large badger burrow. One of the young men was leaning on a long iron digging bar. The other young man held the captive badger by the neck with giant, metal tongs specially designed for the evil purpose. The badger, a large, beautiful creature with that distinctive white stripe running from its nose down its body, was screaming terribly.

The noise made my blood curdle. The badger was turning and twisting as it fought frantically with its long claws. No matter how hard it tried, it couldn't escape the vise-like hold of the tongs around its neck.

"Hold it steady," said the older man. "That's it." He stood still, his feet braced wide apart, holding a pair of fawn-colored dogs on leashes. These sleek, beautiful dogs were taking turns savaging the completely helpless badger.

We stared in horror. We'd heard of badger baiting but this was the first time we'd seen it in action. It was an illegal practice being stamped out by Irish authorities, but some farmers kept doing it because they believed badgers brought disease to their cattle. They also thought that the giant burrows—called sets—risked snapping the legs of their stock if they stepped in them. What shocked me most was the placid way the three men watched as the two dogs assaulted the badger.

"Oh, my God," breathed John in horror.

One dog had the badger by the throat; the other was trying to find a way of ripping open its belly.

"Hey!" Andrew yelled in fury.

The three men turned and stared at us in surprise.

"Leave that badger alone!" screamed John.

"Or we're going to report you!" shouted Andrew.

I was too paralyzed to move and could only stare at the poor creature, unable to say anything like my mouth was wired shut. The unnecessary brutality of it, the complete unfairness of the fight, sickened me so much I thought I was going to vomit. I shook myself.

"Stop doing that, you bastards!" I yelled.

The three men simply tipped their heads back and laughed lazily.

"Let that badger go," I yelled. "Now!"

"Get lost or we'll set the dogs on ye," snapped the older man.

A red mist came over me. "I might not be able to escape my own floggings but that badger fucking well is," I said grimly to Andrew and John. What would Cuchulainn, the warrior boy, have done in this situation? I looked around for a weapon, reached down, and picked up a good-sized rock. Roaring my head off, I ran at the men, and threw the rock at the closest sneering O'Brien head.

"Fuck!" The man dropped the bar and grabbed his nose as blood spurted out. He looked at his hands in shock and saw how much blood there was. "Cheeky little bastard! I'll kill you for that!" He ran straight for me.

I bent down, grabbed another rock, and threw it at him. It bounced right off his forehead.

"Ugh!" He stumbled, his eyes wide with shock.

I might have been skinny, but I could draw blood the same as any grown man.

Wrapping the leashes hard around their forearms, Andrew and John joined me, and side by side, we launched a steady barrage at the three men.

The young man holding the heavy pincers dropped them to protect his head, which allowed the badger to shake itself free. It waddled swiftly into the bushes. We cheered.

The old man shook his fist at us. He could barely restrain his own dogs from fleeing. They were confused about what was happening and just wanted to get out of there, poor things. Major and Rex were going wild on the end of their leashes.

"I'll get you, you little fuckers!" the old man screamed. "I know who you are! You're those bloody Faul freaks."

The two younger men spat on the ground. "And when Dad's finished with you, we'll take our turns," shouted one of them. "What you three little freaks need is a good lesson in manners."

"Yeah? Better get in and make it quick because we'll be reporting you for badger baiting, you cowardly scum!" Andrew yelled back.

They jeered but we walked off, our heads held high. The three of us had saved the badger, and Major and Rex had saved us. It was one of our best battles yet.

"Good dogs," praised John and Andrew, rubbing Major and Rex on the shoulders in gratitude.

However, as we walked back through the trees, I shivered. The O'Briens were adult men and, to be honest, they scared me. Sometimes I wished we weren't so reckless, but what else could we have done? Let the badger be ripped apart while we watched and said nothing?

I bit my lip nervously. We had so many enemies now, they'd have to form a long line and wait their turn if they wanted revenge. The O'Briens, however, were the sort of enemies we could have done without.

"Don't worry. As long as the three of us are together and we've got the dogs, we're safe," I muttered under my breath to myself. "With Major and Rex at our side, we're invincible."

"What's that?" asked Andrew.

I hesitated, not wanting to sound like a coward. "Nothing."

But I still felt uneasy. Was it possible to make too many enemies standing up for your beliefs?

CHAPTER 12

My Patch

AFTER I RAN AWAY, I FOUND I WAS STILL MAKING ENEMIES. As the weather turned colder, I became much more territorial of my patch. Other kids in the area were robbing food from farms, so farmers had zero tolerance to any strays lurking about. "What are you doing around here?" I yelled at any kid wandering past on the track. They'd see me and my six dogs and run for their lives. One boy even shouted, "Fuck off, freak! Don't eat me!" I guess I must have looked more feral than usual.

The area around Padraig's barn was *my* patch, and there was only room for one kid—*me*. My territory covered about twenty farms. I also considered the wealthy Castletroy Estate mine. I had to share the Garryowen Estate with other kids, but secretly I thought of that as mine, too.

I knew if more boys moved into my patch, the farmers would start calling the Gardaí to come catch us. Living rough as I did, the courts would call me uncontrollable. They'd have me dragged off to Borstal's Boys Reform Home. Rumored to be Hell on earth, it was the one place I was absolutely terrified of. If you were sent to Borstal's, you were locked up behind a high, razor-topped fence. There was no way of escaping from the inevitable bullying. Worse yet, everyone knew what went on in places like that.

Several times I was caught stealing food red-handed by farmers. Some farmers, like old psycho Gallagher, were so crazy I'd rather they called the Gardaí than deal with me themselves. One day, happy as a lark, I slipped into Gallagher's henhouse for dinner. I thought he'd gone out for the day but he'd become suspicious and parked his car down the lane so he could sneak up on me.

It was dusty in the henhouse. Downy feathers floated dreamily through the air. Hens looked at me curiously from their nesting boxes and clucked in protest as my fingers reached under them and drew out their toasty warm eggs. I took five eggs from five hens and slipped them in my pocket. *Excellent. That's dinner sorted.* I was about to reach for just one more when I felt something metal-hard prodding my spine. I froze.

Old Gallagher had a voice like bent nails. "Put 'em back." I heard the safety of his double-barrel shotgun click off. "Put 'em back. Or I'll blow a hole in yer so big a cow could walk through it."

I slowly put the egg in my hand back in the nest.

"And the others."

I carefully pulled the eggs from my pockets and placed them under the same hen. She clucked gently at the touch of my fingers. I felt gut-churning ashamed to be treated as less than an animal. Less than a chicken.

He prodded me in the spine. "Get going. If I see yer back here, I'll shoot yer."

I didn't believe every farmer who made that threat, but I believed old Gallagher. As I walked past him, I couldn't stop the tears from coming.

I never returned to old psycho Gallagher's farm. Civilization didn't exist in that place.

———

My run-in with Gallagher got me thinking later that night. As I curled up in the warm hay in Padraig's barn, I stared up at the tin ceiling. For the first time I fully realized how lucky I was to have the run of this lovely, peaceful farm.

Padraig now knew I lived here. Being an old bachelor and kind, he left me alone as long as I stayed out of sight and kept my dogs under control. Often I caught myself thinking, *Thanks, Padraig. I'll never forget how kind you are.* Now I'd have to be especially careful not to annoy him. A place as good as this would be hard to find if I got kicked out.

A few days later I was walking back to Padraig's along the raised railway line when I unexpectedly came across a local gang of kids. They were crawling out of a hole in the farm hedge, sucking raw eggs and laughing.

I stared, enraged. That was *my* farm! Those were *my* eggs! I glanced behind me. Where the hell were my dogs?

I knew these boys. They were the McDonaghs—seven tough kids from a tough family. Their dad was a brutal man and a real hard drinker. Both parents were rumored to be laid out flat on their backs unconscious with drink by ten in the morning almost every day. As a result some of the younger kids had formed a gang and were now running pretty feral.

Warily, I walked towards them and found myself facing Anky, Decky, Fonan, Boyd, Grub, Seamus, and String.

Bloody hell. They looked even wilder than me. Their clothes were ragged, their hair was wild, and their eyes flickered over me and everything else. All of them were carrying big blackthorn sticks with razor-sharp barbs. They moved in closer until they were shoulder to shoulder.

Their head boy, Anky, flipped his chin at me. "Come 'ere, I want ya, sham," he yelled. His accent was real working-class Limerick. It meant, *Come here, I want you, person.* It was rude the way he said it.

I stayed where I was. "This is all *my* territory," I yelled back. "You'd better leave."

Anky raised his chin again. "Fuck ya. Yer one of them Faullies. The freaky moron one. Hangs with the dogs. Well, I don't see na dogs."

I ignored him. "Listen. This is my patch. From the Grudie swimming holes to Rhebogue gypsy camp and all the farms in between. Castletroy Estate's mine too."

"Yeah?" he said with a laugh. "Well, there's only one of ye and seven of us, and we all have sticks." He spat on the ground at his feet. "So ye listen to me, yer little skinny fucker. Whatever we McDonaghs want, we take." The brothers looked at each other and smiled. Then with blood-curdling screams, all seven ran straight at me.

Shit. Should I stay or run? If I wanted to keep my territory, I had to stand and fight. What was my fight strategy? *Grab a blackthorn stick off one of them. String looks the weakest.*

I started hollering at the top of my voice as I ran at String. His mouth went round with shock when I tackled him to the ground. I sat astride his skinny stomach and grabbed at the blackthorn stick. My palms and fingers instantly burst out in pain. Wide-eyed with panic, String clutched the smooth handle of the stick to his chest for dear life.

The rest of the gang descended on me. Blackthorn sticks rained down on my head vicious and fast. Razor stripes of pain ripped across my bare skin, across the back of my head and face, and especially my hands and back. The barbs of a blackthorn stick were hideous bastard things. They snagged at my skin and ripped clean through each time the sticks were yanked away.

One thing I had in my favor was that I was so used to getting beaten by my teachers and by my dad. I was also used to getting whacked hard in hurling matches, which meant I wasn't scared of pain. It was just a matter of seeing how much I could endure before I gave up. Triumphantly, I yanked the stick free from String's fingers. *Yes!* Now I had a weapon! The fight was about to get a little more interesting.

I climbed to my feet and faced them. Blood dripped down my face and I wiped it away with the back of my wrist.

We all went a bit crazy then, the seven McDonaghs and me going at it hammer and tong with our blackthorn sticks, half trying to kill each other. It was probably a lot of pent up anger needing to find release. We were just kids trying to survive, a lost generation affected by our fathers' alcoholism.

There were too many boys to fight, and I soon sank to my haunches, my chest heaving.

Anky lifted his head. He was bent over, panting hard too. He rubbed away blood dripping into his eye and nodded his chin at me. "Git 'im now while he's down, boys. Come on!"

I knew they'd beaten me raw this time around because I could feel a sugar crash coming on. I was too exhausted to care if I lost or not.

Suddenly I heard barking. My dogs were running towards us, all six of them, galloping hard, heads low, hackles up, teeth on display. They obviously didn't like the look of so many boys with sticks around me.

"Fuckin' mongrels!" screamed Anky. He held up his stick and backed away a few steps, swiping at them with big, wild swings.

Blackie took an instant dislike to him. He lowered his huge, shaggy lion's head at the boy's legs, trying to bite the back of his calves. Anky shrieked for his brothers to help then yelled at me. "Call off yer fuckin' dog, Faul!"

"Blackie," I croaked. I was too exhausted to do anything.

Meanwhile Fergus darted at String. "Bugger this for a joke! I'm fuckin' outta here," the boy yelled and bolted off like a skinny hare, with Fergus yapping hard at his ankles.

The other brothers glanced wildly at Anky. He was swinging his stick as the big black monster of a Newfoundland was stalking him. The boys looked at my other dogs advancing on them.

"You can keep yer stupid barn!" Fonan yelled over his shoulder. "And yer fucking eggs!" He picked up his stick and bolted. His brothers—all but Anky—followed.

Anky was still being pursued by Blackie. The boy backed away, every now and again swinging wildly at the huge dog who was still circling him. "Fuck yer, Faullie! I swear I'll git yer for this!" Dodging around Blackie, he ran after his brothers down the railway line.

The dogs chased him a bit, just for fun. Then they trotted back to me with their tails high in the air like victory flags. I rolled on my back in agony and groaned while they licked and sniffed me all over, fascinated by so much blood. "Thanks dogs, but what on earth took you so long?"

Later, after I got some food in me, I took the dogs down to the Grudie. This was the secluded swimming hole just off the Shannon River. We celebrated our triumph with a swim. Even

Blackie jumped in. We really felt like the Dirty Dog Gang now after trouncing the McDonagh Gang.

———

After that fight, I kept a blackthorn stick at my side to protect me from the McDonaghs and any other gangs I might come across. The fight reminded me how lucky I was to have the dogs with me. That night I rubbed their ears as we lazed about in the hay in Padraig's barn. "Wouldn't be easy living rough if I didn't have you lot to protect my back," I told them gratefully.

It was true. With the dogs at my side, I could walk freely around the area. I slept safely at night. Best of all, my dogs had such positive energy they kept me happy and confident. With them around, I felt invincible. They were my family. My friends. My gang. They were everything to me.

People did try to separate us. There were times when I was caught and dragged home by well-meaning neighbors, and a few times even by old Father Ray, the priest. My mammy begged them to help get me home. But as soon as I was dragged inside the house and locked in my bedroom, I'd feel claustrophobic and needed to escape.

Mammy pleaded with me to stay through the locked bedroom door. "Please, Marcine! *Pleease!* I need to know you're safe!"

I genuinely didn't want to break her heart, but I'd changed too much. After the freedom of the barn and the calmness of being around my gang of dogs, I couldn't accept any more of my father's erratic behavior. And as for ever going back to school—ha! *Forget it.* They'd have to drag me dead back inside that sadistic place.

I couldn't ever get back to my barn fast enough. As soon as I heard the key turn in the lock of the bedroom door, I'd climb out the window, shimmy down the pipe, and run down the road, shutting my ears to the heartbreaking sounds of Mammy crying and calling after me, "Please, Marcine. *I love you!* Come back! *Please!*" I knew if I stayed at home, I wouldn't survive. It was simple as that.

I wouldn't rest until I reached the railway line. As soon as my feet touched the big wooden girders and metal rails of the tracks, my heart stopped thudding and I started breathing easier. I was safely back in *my* territory now.

The dogs would run out of the blackberry bushes to greet me ecstatically and dance around me with their tongues hanging out. *You're back! You're back! You made it back to us safely!*

The dogs had taught me what real freedom tasted like and what pure happiness felt like. They loved me just as I was. I couldn't give up any of those things, not even for Mammy. So, I stuffed all thoughts of her away into the dark, back cupboard of my heart.

I hadn't cut myself off entirely from people, however. I learned the importance of human friendship when my brothers introduced me to Brandon Ryan, the boy who'd become my best friend and change my life forever. One day he walked up the railway line with my brothers on one of their visits to check on me. Andrew and John had a special way of finding me. They used what we called the "Indian holler" we'd seen and heard in Hollywood movies. You'd tilt your chin back, bang your palm against your mouth, and yell at the top of your lungs, "Woa-woa-woa-woa-woa-woa!"

There was always a bit of an Irish accent lurking around the edges we couldn't get rid of, but it still worked. If I heard them, I'd holler back. The dogs loved it and went crazy with barking.

At first I was a bit wary of Brandon but it didn't take long to trust him, which was very unusual for me. He went to St. Johns school on the other side of Garryowen. That's why I'd never met him before.

"Hi ya, Martin," he said. "I'm Brandon. Fancy a smoke?" He pulled out precious cigarettes for the four of us.

I was impressed by his generosity and took one. "Thanks."

He grinned. "No problem."

I felt my ADHD, which usually went wild around new kids, go quietly to sleep.

The four of us chatted for a while. When Brandon left with Andrew and John a few hours later, I watched them walk down the line together. Strange. I wasn't even envious of him spending time with my brothers. He was too nice to hate.

A few days later I heard more "Indian hollering" coming up the railway. "Woa-woa-woa-woa-woa-woa!" I whistled up the dogs and went to meet them, but it was just Brandon this time. My first instinct was to bolt.

The truth was, I was painfully shy and I had no idea of what to say to him. I thought it would be much better just to hide in the bushes and wait for him to get bored and go home.

"Martin! For fuck's sakes!" he yelled as I skidded down the embankment. "Don't run off. I'm knackered. Here, sit down and have a cigarette," he panted.

I sat down beside him on the tracks. The dogs wandered around us, shoving themselves in for pats and to sniff Brandon all over. We smoked in companionable silence for a while, rubbing the dogs behind their ears.

After a bit he said, "Why are ye living so rough then, Martin? Your brothers seem alright living at home."

My eyes jumped to his. *Shit*. Why did he have to go and spoil things, asking difficult questions? My mouth jammed shut. How could I explain it all? The craziness that came from my ADHD? The insanity that hit our house whenever Dad got drunk? The nightmare situation at school? The relentless teasing and bullying of the kids in our neighborhood? I didn't want him thinking I was a freak. Nervously, I took a drag on my cigarette. "Yeah, I just prefer my independence," I said as casually as I could. "That's all, and I like living with these dogs. Can't keep them at home."

He blew a plume of smoke out his nose and nodded. He was a sensitive kid and was quickly realizing he'd just stepped on uncomfortable territory. "Yeah. Bet it's nice and quiet out here. I've got sixteen brothers and sisters. Wouldn't mind escaping from that mad lot sometimes, I can tell you."

I laughed. My stomach rumbled and I flicked him a sideways glance.

"How about we drop past my place?" he said. "See if I can find us something to eat?"

I agreed. I have to admit, it was now very strange for me to be walking through the middle of the Garryowen Estate in broad daylight.

When we came to Brandon's front door, he turned to me and said, "Wait!" He listened carefully and then murmured over his shoulder, "Won't be long now. I'll have to try to get you past my dad. Get ready to dive inside when I give the word."

"Dinner!" a voice yelled from inside. "First lot!" An avalanche of young kids came crashing down the staircase, shoving and pushing past us noisily on their way through to the kitchen.

"Quick, Martin! This is our chance!" Brandon hissed. I followed fast on his heels.

We paused on the kitchen threshold. Squashed around the kitchen table must have been ten kids, all happily talking at the top of their voices. A lady who must've been Mrs. Ryan was serving up a stew. It smelt delicious. Brandon yanked me by the arm to follow him inside.

Suddenly a hand descended on my head, and before I could blink I was being propelled towards the front door. It was Brandon's dad.

"Whoa! You're not one of mine, young fella. Out you go. Sorry but I've got enough mouths to feed in here."

Brandon was pushed gently back inside. "Sorry, Martin!" he yelled over his shoulder. "Wait for me at the gate." He was quickly enveloped in the noisy, happy crowd around the table.

I waited on his front brick wall, feeling like a dog who'd been tied up outside.

After thirty minutes, he reappeared. "Sorry about that. With so many kids in the family, we have three sittings for dinner." He shrugged. "Didn't know Dad would be guarding the door tonight. Kids from the neighborhood have been sneaking in for a free meal, so Dad's started doing random head checks." He pulled out a big slice of soda bread. "But I managed to grab this, butter it, *and* dip it in gravy."

My stomach nearly wept with joy. "Thanks," I said, and by Jesus, I meant it. It was a thoughtful gift from my first real friend. And someone who wasn't a brother or a dog.

It was Brandon's idea to get me a job delivering coal door-to-door for the Donoghues. They were a miserable, sour family, and only one brother bothered inspecting me when Brandon dragged me along for the job interview.

"This is Billy. He makes all the decisions," whispered Brandon.

I felt like I was at the Garryowen Horse Fair, only this time, I was the horse. I almost neighed in his face, but Brandon's pleading eyes stopped me.

"Don't look too trustworthy to me," Billy said to Brandon, looking me up and down in distaste as he circled us.

Yeah, and you look like a real charming fellow, too, I thought. I pasted a fake smile on my face and said, "My name is Martin, sir."

Brandon gestured grandiloquently at me and went straight into his sales pitch. "Na, na. You've got him all wrong, sir. Sure, he's a grand fella. Very polite. Good with customers. Wonderful with the horses. He knows all the streets around here. Knows the houses well."

Yeah. Only because I go through their trash scavenging for food.

Brandon looked at me, silently imploring me to behave.

"A job'd be very much appreciated, sir," I said insincerely.

"A 'right," Billy grunted. "You're hired." He started walking away, muttering over his shoulder, "If yer break the cart or a hoss, I'll flog yer raw me self."

I bowed and tugged an imaginary cap behind his back. "Oh, *thank you* so much. You're really kind, sir."

Brandon kicked my foot, then dragged me down the road to see the horses. "Jesus, Martin. Can't you just play the game when you need to?"

"I'm trying," I protested, but secretly, I knew I'd always rebel when people with power tried to bully me. I couldn't help it. I'd always fight back until my last dying breath. No one was ever going to bully me again.

The Donoghues' horses were huge, well-muscled, and beautiful creatures, which were kept on the common land owned by the council a few streets away. "Every morning we work, we have to come here and grab our horse," Brandon explained. He walked up to a giant pie-bald. "We have Neddy here. I've been using him for a while and he's a grand old fella, aren't yer boy?"

The horse turned to look at us in boredom then resumed grazing. *Yeah, yeah, kids, leave me alone. I've got grass to eat.*

My first morning working with Brandon went off without a hitch. Well, almost. I arrived at the common to find Brandon hopping mad and no Neddy. "What's wrong?" I asked.

He was enraged. "Those bloody McDonald bastard kids moved Neddy last night! To the other side of Garryowen! Did it deliberately!"

"Why would they do that?"

Brandon spat on the ground in disgust. "Means they want to get a head start on us so they can steal our customers. Hurry up! We're gonna have to run or we'll make no money today."

We bolted through the empty streets of Garryowen to the field on the other side of the estate. There was Neddy eating peacefully. Brandon jammed a carrot in his surprised mouth, chucked a rope around his neck, and started hauling him down the road. "Neddy, please don't piss about today. Just wait 'til I get my hands on those sly rat McDonalds."

I'd never seen Brandon so angry.

We hurried to the Donoghues' yard. "Yer late," snapped Billy and jerked his thumb at a big pile of coal sacks and the other fuel lying in the corner. "There yer go. Start loading."

I felt a bit sorry for the horse when I saw the pile. Poor Neddy had to pull *all* that? Soon I transferred my pity to Brandon and me. While Neddy stood about lazily watching, we struggled to load twenty-five bags of coal, eight bags of wooden blocks, and five bales of peat brickettes. At last the twenty-foot wooden cart was loaded.

"Come on!" shouted Brandon. He jumped up on the cart and clicked and whooped until Neddy pulled away, flicking his tail in irritation at all the yelling.

I jumped up beside Brandon and held on tight. When Neddy started trotting, I thought we'd be shaken to death as we got up to speed. My teeth were rattling in my head. Once we were on the smooth tarmac it was much better.

Neddy pulled the cart along effortlessly. It felt like sailing. Brandon was like a boy possessed. "Keep an eye out for those McDonalds!" he yelled.

We were soon swinging into the perfectly manicured lawns of the Castletroy Estate. I was usually hiding behind cars and bushes whenever I was in this neighborhood, but now I sat tall, enjoying my high perch in full view as we whizzed along. People waved at us in their dressing gowns as they came out to fetch their milk and bread. Brandon was obviously well liked.

"Hello, Brandon! Drop around after breakfast and we'll buy a bag."

"No problem, Mrs. Clare! See yer soon."

We took another corner fast and headed for the wealthiest street of all. Mercedes and Jaguars were pulling out of driveways. The drivers waved at Brandon.

"Why does everyone like you so much?" I asked in amazement. I'd never seen so many people wave at a boy before.

"Because I smile and I'm not a cheeky fuck like you," he replied. He hunched over to concentrate as we swung onto the wealthiest street of all. Immediately, he started cursing.

On the opposite end of the street was another coal cart racing straight towards us at a real, spanking trot. Two ratty-looking boys held on for dear life. They started throwing insults as soon as they saw us.

"I'll kill those McDonalds one day," growled Brandon. "It's bloody Dermot and his younger brother." He slid closer to the edge of the cart, and crouched down, ready to jump. He handed me the reins. "Martin, ready? Guard the horse and cart while I run up and knock on the door. The lady knows me but I've got to get to her first." He leapt from the cart while I pulled Neddy to a stop. I watched him run across the perfect lawn at the same time Dermot McDonald sprinted up the path.

Neck and neck, both dashed up the stone-flagged path to the porch and front door. Brandon suddenly swerved, shoved Dermot hard, and kept running. Dermot cursed as he tripped and rolled across the grass.

Brandon reached the big front door, rang the buzzer and doubled over, panting. I lit up a cigarette to watch the show.

Brandon straightened up the instant the door opened. "Good morning, Mrs. Healey. Would you like to buy some coal today?"

"Oh, lovely, Brandon! Let me get my purse." She disappeared inside.

Dermot McDonald slunk back down the path, holding his elbow, limping a little. He spat on the road as he passed by. "Fuck ya, Faullie."

Raising my cigarette to him, I replied, "Morning, Dermot."

From the porch, Brandon stuck his thumb up in victory. We had our first customer of the day.

Brandon and I made a great team. It was hard slog doing coal deliveries but we sure had lots of laughs together. He showed me the delivery business, and I showed him how to make friends with the neighborhood dogs, especially the tricky ones.

Dogs loved jumping up on him as he carried the heavy bags of coal into their backyards. I taught him a few helpful dog signals to prevent this. "Completely ignore the dog and raise your chin as you march straight past, even if it tries to block you," I told him. "Think calm, boring thoughts because dogs smell fear as easily as humans smell bleach. Act with purpose and show no hesitation."

"Okay."

"When you do this you're saying in dog language, *Please leave me alone, I'm busy doing a job here.*"

Sometimes I shared my theories with the customers. One day, a yellow Labrador ran out at us, barking aggressively at Neddy's legs. Neddy swung his head around and looked at me as if to say, *Do something, kid.*

I walked up to the door, ignoring the silly bugger of a dog with my arms crossed and chin up. I was totally relaxed so all the dog could smell was my calmness and confidence. I continued ignoring the dog while it barked at me and rang the doorbell until the owner answered it.

I smiled politely. "Excuse me, missus, but your dog is frightening the horse. Nearly bit his leg."

The lady was very apologetic. It seems that most Irish people love horses. "Oh dear, I don't know how to stop Sandy. He's so naughty these days."

"I know what's happening," I said helpfully. "Sandy's problem is he keeps scent-marking across the road." She looked at me in surprise. I wasn't your normal coal delivery boy.

"He'll do it especially in the mornings and evenings," I continued. "If you join up all those spots he pisses, you can see he's making an invisible smell fence. He's working hard to make your property bigger so now he thinks he owns the middle of the road, too."

"Oh, yes, I *have* seen Sandy widdling across the street quite a bit."

"In the dog world, the more you piss—I mean *widdle*—on it, you more you own it," I said. "He'll chase anyone who comes along and invades his part of the road. I don't want Sandy mauling poor Neddy's legs."

"Oh, dear me, no. But what can I do? The front fence is so low. He jumps it whenever he wants."

I knew how to fix that, too. "Keep him in the backyard. It'll take him off guard duty and he won't be able to jump that fence. It's too high. When you take him for a walk, keep him on his leash, and drag him past his scent-marking spots."

She thanked me and dragged a very surprised Sandy inside by the collar. I ran back to the coal cart.

Brandon grinned. "I think you might be a natural-born teacher, Martin."

My mouth dropped open. Me? A teacher? Now *that* was crazy.

Brandon taught me other things—like how to charm customers. His father owned a second-hand furniture store and had passed his natural salesman talents on to his son. Brandon made it all sound so easy. "Just be genuinely nice," he suggested. "Have manners and be pleasant. Yes, I'm afraid that *will* involve smiling, Martin."

I dropped my insolence and cheekiness and practiced smiling, which felt very unnatural at first. I mixed this with a few things I'd learned about charm from my father when he was sober. Soon I was even impressing myself.

The ferocious scowl I'd traditionally greeted people with was replaced by an open smile and welcoming eyes. In the beginning, I only thought of the money I'd make, but after a while I discovered I actually enjoyed making people happy.

It was intoxicating. "Ah, Mrs. Neal, you sure look very pretty today. Would you like a little extra coal for your shed? I could carry some inside if you like. Save you doing it."

"Thank you, dear. What a lovely lad you are."

"See?" laughed Brandon as we drove Neddy to the next house. "You're not as unlikable as you think you are."

I realized he was right. I was starting to like the new me.

My dogs liked the new me as well.

They weren't as pushy as they used to be now that I was happy. My happiness added maybe hundreds of points to my daily point score. They moved about the barn much more calmly. If I was relaxed, they were relaxed.

"Good dogs," I found myself constantly saying. To make my praise mean even more, I would slowly close my eyes and breathe deeply. This, I had discovered, was dog language for *Well done*.

This change in their behavior helped me understand why the dogs had thrown so many challenges at me in the past: An unhappy human can't be trusted to be in charge of the pack. Any time the dogs sensed I was emotionally vulnerable, they knew it was time to take over and grab the leadership. It wasn't anything personal; it was just their survival instincts kicking into action.

The day someone stole a precious new blanket Brandon had given me was one such moment. Or when I glimpsed Mammy driving by on her way to work. Such things could shatter my peace and within minutes, I'd become an emotional mess.

The dogs would flick me a glance that said, *Sorry kid, but you can't be trusted to be making the right decisions for the rest of us, not in this mood.* Then they'd start testing each other and me, and the game would be back on again. There'd be more pushing and shoving, barking and manic behavior. They'd start trying to invade my personal space again.

If I was really angry or moody, they usually went quiet, but their rising tension was impossible to ignore. "Oh, stop tiptoeing around like some creeping Jesus!" I'd snap irritably. "Go lie down and stop bothering me!"

Each dog reacted differently to my stress. Fergus and Red paced around and panted while watching me out of the corner of their eyes. Missy and Blackie slunk away. Pa and Mossy would lay down in corners, facing away from me, their chins on the ground, trying to shut me out in the most neutral way they could.

A loud stressed sigh from the lot of them would bring me back to how tense the dogs were. "I'm sorry, dogs. I mean it. I'm really sorry. Just a bit of a bad day today and I stupidly took it out on you poor things."

It was easy to tell when I was genuinely calm again; I only had to check how the dogs were behaving. The dogs sensed the moment I could be trusted to be in charge again. They'd yawn or shake any lingering tension off then roll over and go to sleep to neutralize the stress that had been flying around the barn.

I'd look around at them and feel guilty. *Poor bastards.* Dogs are like sponges, soaking up our human energy. Our bad energy as well as our good energy. It made me realize there were three important gifts we should constantly bring home for our dogs. Happiness. Calmness. Optimism.

Food for their souls, not for just their stomachs.

CHAPTER 13

Dirty War

THE NIGHTMARE I HAD ONE NIGHT WHILE STILL AT HOME felt freakishly real. In it, the two O'Brien brothers were laughing as they hunted me down relentlessly. Their father yelled after me, "If ye care about bloody badgers so much, we'll treat yer like one, eh?"

Panicking, I ran panting through the trees until I fell into a badger hole. The three men stood grinning down at me. Dirt spilled over the edge into my eyes. "Not so tough now are you, kid, without yer brothers and dogs to protect ye?"

I looked up at them completely terrified.

They grinned. "Here's a little Garryowen gift for yer, boy. Payback for those rocks yer threw at us." With a whoop, they sent their two dogs down after me.

Screaming, I tried to escape but heavy badger tongs closed around my neck and held me trapped. I stared up in horror. One of the O'Brien brothers lazily raised his shotgun, aimed straight at my face, and shot me point blank. I sat up screaming with my heart hammering like a wild thing.

"Shut up, Martin," moaned Andrew.

I woke up and found myself on the floor, tangled in my blanket, panting in fear, clammy with sweat. It was morning and I'd wet the bed again. This was my most shameful secret.

170

I was completely terrified the kids at school would learn of it. John, Andrew, and I had had to share a bed until I started pissing myself. From that point on, we agreed I'd sleep on the floor. This was much better for everyone because then I didn't feel so guilty. I just had to air out my own blankets every morning and wash them when I could.

I rubbed my face, desperately trying to erase the last bits of my fear too. Most of the time I did my best to forget the enemies I'd made around Garryowen, but while I slept they came looking for me and usually found me. The O'Brien nightmare was my least favorite.

I crawled out of my blankets to get rid of the stink of urine and get ready for school. So began the horrible day my life started unraveling.

I stumbled downstairs to the kitchen. Mammy was at work, and Dad supervising breakfast.

"Did you wet the bed last night?" he asked.

"Yes," I said, staring down at my cereal bowl. The tension in the room was rising fast. My brothers and sisters fell quiet. Major and Rex slunk out.

"Like a girl?"

"No. Not like a girl. Couldn't help it." I looked at him warily and hunched into myself, humiliated.

"Don't worry. I know how to stop you." Back then it was believed that wetting the bed was simply due to a lack of willpower. There were many suggested cures bandied about by our neighbors, but I was about to discover my dad had come up with his own idea.

He flicked something across the table at me. It bounced off my chest then dropped to my feet. I glanced down. It was a cardboard sign hanging from a necklace of string. "Put it on."

I looked at it blankly.

"Since you can't read it," he said. "I'll read it for you. 'I WET MY BED.'"

"I can't wear that," I whispered.

"Oh, yes you can." He waited.

I had no choice. I reached down and hung the sign around my neck. A bit of a sob escaped from my mouth. My brothers and sisters couldn't look at me and kept eating their breakfasts quietly.

"Come with me," my dad ordered.

My eyes widened. "What do I have to do?"

Dad smiled. "Since you keep deliberately wetting the bed for attention, let's go." He gestured to the door. "Hurry up. If it's attention you want, then we'd better make sure you get some."

This was going to be worse than any nightmare. What on earth did he have in mind? I followed him upstairs and watched as he picked up my wet mattress and threw it straight down the staircase. Then I followed him as he dragged it down the hall, out the front door, up the path, and through our gate.

I was numb with fear.

"Here they come," said my dad in satisfaction. "The first lot of kids on their way to school."

I tried to shut my ears off and stared hard at the pavement. My face and ears were burning hot. *This isn't happening. This isn't happening.* I wanted to die but this nightmare was real and I couldn't get away. I glanced sideways and saw my mattress on the concrete path. It reeked of urine. *Please let me die.*

The kids' voices were loud and clear. "Oh my God, that's one of the Faullie triplets. The weird one! What's the sign say 'round his neck? Wait 'til everyone at school hears about this!"

I heard my dad say cheerfully, "This is Martin, my son. Yes, as you can see, he wets the bed. Bad as a baby." He folded his arms. "Maybe now he'll bother using the toilet at night like everyone else in the family."

There was laughter and jeers and the sound of lazy spitting. I couldn't even raise my chin in defiance. Why didn't I just run away?

I guess I realized there was no escape. Everyone in the entire school would know soon enough. Even if I did run, God only knew what my father would do next. Drag the mattress down to the school gates? Bring it into my classroom? Probably.

I'd never hated him more. After all the kids had walked by, I tore the cardboard sign from my neck that I couldn't even read and dragged myself up to my room to get changed for school. I was in a dangerous mood.

—◆—

Of course, the kids at school made life hell for me that day. By lunchtime I was wild when a crowd of boys gathered around me in the schoolyard.

"Anyone got a nappy? Hurry, we need a nappy for Faullie over here."

"*Phew!* I can smell pissy wee-wee on the big pissy baby."

All the kids were laughing and staring at me with sharp, mocking eyes. I tried to switch it off, but the kids kept tormenting until I was getting into fights, left and right. Andrew and John tried to help, but I shoved them off angrily.

Right after lunch I was feeling so volatile that I thought I would explode. I sat at my desk with my arms folded and chin high.

Mr. Keeley smirked at me. Someone must have told him all about it but instead of raising the subject, he decided to prod at another tender spot of mine. He gave us a writing exercise. "I'll give you ten minutes. Time begins . . . now."

Of course, my paper remained blank and my arms stayed crossed. I hadn't even bothered picking up my pen.

He smiled at me. "Time is . . . up." Keeley walked towards me. "Ah, I see you've done *sterling* work there, Faul. *Magnificent.* Absolutely nothing. Not one word have you written. Surely you could have managed your name? Let me help you." He looked around the class happily as everyone but Andrew, John, and I obediently tittered. "Ready? Faul is spelled S . . . T . . . U . . . P . . . I . . . D."

The class roared with laughter except my brothers and me. John and Andrew sat silently enraged but helpless. I exploded and swung my chair up, hitting Keeley across the head.

He went completely ballistic and shoved me out of the room like a mad man before he killed me.

From that day on, we loathed each other beyond words.

❦

There was more punishment to come when Headmaster Crowe visited our class one day. He said something to Mr. Keeley, and they both laughed and came over to my desk. Their smiles were ugly things.

"Mr. Faul," Crowe crowed. "I'm afraid you've failed to complete the required studies for this grade," he said, staring down at me. "I'm afraid if you wish to graduate from St. Patrick's, then you'll have to re-take classes until you can read and write to an appropriate standard."

This was new. When had they ever given a damn about my education before? I'd always thought they'd be glad to see the back of me. My brothers looked on helplessly.

"Please pack up your things and come this way. You'll have to repeat all the grades until you achieve minimum reading and writing skills," he said with a smirk. "In fact, we have a nice desk waiting for you in the baby class."

Baby class? That was what we called kindergarten. I'd never heard of anyone having to repeat the whole of primary school before. "You can't make me," I croaked.

"Then tell us where you hid the Pope's money," said Crowe, leaning closer, hands on my desk. His eyes gleamed straight into mine.

Shit, I'd spent it already. There was nothing left. I knew it wouldn't matter whether or not I told him where the Pope's money was. These two men were determined to break me. Once that happened, I knew I was a goner.

"Do you know what I *really* hate? Bullies," I said loudly and clearly. "And I swear this—no teacher is going to break me. *Ever.*"

Crowe's eyes narrowed. He forced himself to take a long, slow breath. "Very well, then. Come along, Faul. You've obviously made your choice."

Together Crowe and Keeley walked me down the corridor. I tried to act as though I didn't care but this new humiliation cut deep, as they knew it would. I stubbornly held my chin a bit higher in defiance.

Half way down the corridor, reality hit me. *My brothers were going to graduate at the end of the year without me.* While they moved on to high school, I'd still be at St. Patrick's in baby class.

This was my private version of Hell: me stuck in this hated place forever while the teachers gleefully made me repeat all the grades again and again. By God, I'd die of old age before anyone in this place ever managed to teach me to read or write.

I swallowed hard. *Whatever happens,* I told myself, *don't cry.*

The two bastard teachers on either side of me talked happily over my head, but I shut them out. All I saw out of the corner of my eye were their mouths opening and shutting. Keeley was clearly enjoying himself immensely as he opened the door to a classroom and gestured me inside.

Twenty terrified kids were staring at me. They were all tiny with big round eyes nailed to me like I was a huge gorilla who was invading their room.

"Here's your new chair, Mr. Faul," Keeley said, pulling out a tiny wooden chair. It looked like it belonged in a doll house. "Please sit."

I don't know why, but I obeyed him. I guess it was shock.

"Enjoy yourself," he said and turned towards the door. "Don't despair. You may find you understand everything a little better the *second* time around. Or maybe it'll sink in the *third* time around. Not to worry—I'll be here for years and years to come."

I ground my teeth together so hard they hurt. He turned his back on me and started talking to Crowe.

The kindergarten teacher was sitting behind his desk. He stood up and walked to the front of the room, clapping his hands bossily. "Right. Now that little show is over, who can tell me what sound these two letters make when you put them together?" He pointed at the chalkboard. "S-H." He cupped a hand to his ear. "*Shhhhh.* Good. Can everyone repeat that? *Shhhhh.* Excellent. Now who can tell me some words that start with *Shhhhh?*"

I stared down at my knuckles. I was clenching them so tight, they glowed pure white. I felt a sudden wave of fury sweep over me.

"Yes, that's right. *Shell*," said the teacher slowly. "*Sheep. Shake. Ship. Shine. Shoe. Shadow . . .*"

Suddenly, like I was just waking up, I muttered, "Why the fuck am I sitting here?"

The words dropped into the hushed room like rocks.

The teacher stopped and frowned, unable to believe his ears. "I beg your pardon, Faul?" Keeley and Crowe turned and stared at me, their eyes narrowing fast.

This was it. I had to decide what happened next. Was I going to keep putting up with this abuse? It obviously was never going to stop. Or was I going to escape?

"Fuck this! I'm out of here!" I yelled at the top of my voice. The baby chair fell away with a clatter.

Everyone's mouth dropped open in shock. Keeley's eyes were nearly popping out of his head.

I sprang towards the large open classroom window. The classroom was on the ground floor so there wasn't much of a drop, but I wouldn't have cared how far I had to jump. *I was escaping from fucking school at last!* I started running as soon as I hit the ground. Behind me, it was pandemonium.

Crowe, Keeley, and the kindergarten teacher were screaming blue murder. Loudest of all were kids from all the classrooms rushing noisily to watch me run away. They roared in approval.

My mind was spinning. Where could I go? It was probably safest to go home. Major and Rex wouldn't let anything bad happen to me. I knew Keeley would be frothing at the mouth to give me the thrashing of my life. He'd most likely chase after me in his car. Right now I didn't care. I was free at last!

When I made it to the house, I discovered that it was locked. I didn't have a key so I unlatched the gate and let myself into our backyard. Major and Rex rushed to greet me, sensing my distress. I gratefully rubbed their ears. "Hello, boys. Good dogs. Nice fellas." Then it sunk in. *What had I just done?*

I sat down on the concrete path, buried my head in my knees, and rocked back and forth. The dogs pushed their noses in and started licking my face. I was too upset to shove them away.

What was I going to do now? I had no idea. *Oh, God, what's Mammy going to say?* I didn't even want to think of my dad's reaction. God only knew what he'd do.

Could those bastard teachers really force me to repeat school until I learned to read and write? One thing was clear. I never wanted to go back to school again. They'd have to put me in a straitjacket and carry me back.

A car pulled up with a screech. I peered over the back fence. It was Keeley and Mr. Rollins, his best friend on the staff. More adrenaline started coursing through me. This time I wasn't going to take their beatings quietly. Not anymore. I would make my stand. I'd always boasted about how much I wanted to be an ancient Celtic warrior. Well, now it was time to man up and fight back.

"Come on dogs," I said, as I walked to the coal shed and flung open the door. I ran my trembling fingers down the handle of my hurley stick. No, not that. Suddenly I knew what to use as weapons. *That* would wake up those two sadistic bastards alright.

I grabbed the choke chains for Major and Rex and slipped them over their noble necks. The three of us began walking towards the side gate. It was time to meet my enemies. "Okay

Major? Rex?" They whined softly. My heart pounded in my chest like a drum and courage welled up within me. With these two magnificent warrior dogs at my side I would surely be invincible.

I could see Keeley's little Fiat parked at the curb. He and Rollins were standing there with weapons in their hands. Keeley, his cosh. Rollins, his leather belt wrapped around his knuckles. These two teachers were so enraged, they didn't care who might see them threatening to beat up a kid in public.

"Faul, get out here right now!" Keeley shouted across the fence at me. "Because I swear I'm going to flog you so hard for this insolence you're not going to be able to sit down for a long time!"

Seeing the cruelty glinting in his eyes, I felt my chin go up. I unlatched the back gate and walked down the side passage straight for the front gate. The teachers spotted Major and Rex on their leashes padding along at my side.

"Put those bloody dogs back in the yard, then get in the car!" Keeley yelled.

Both dogs were pulling on their leashes, growling deeply in their throats. I kept walking, my eyes never leaving Keeley or Rollins.

"Stop arsing around, Faul!" yelled Rollins, sounding a little nervous. It always spooked teachers when I stared them straight in the eye and remained silent. Now there were two angry German Shepherds staring at them too.

I bent down and tied the dogs' leashes to the small wire fence that ran on either side of the path protecting Mammy's flowers. Tremors quivered through their bodies as they growled, their eyes nailed ferociously on the two men.

Next, I made a deal with myself. If the teachers unlatched my front gate and walked inside, I'd release the dogs. My fingers rubbed the metal clips on their collars in readiness. "You're not taking one step on my property," I said calmly.

Rollins hesitated, but Keeley took one look at the angle of my chin and strode forward. A vein pulsed at his temple as his fingers ran over the gate for the latch. "You're going to regret this, Faul."

"Step inside the gate, and I'll set the dogs on you."

He curled his lip at me. "You wouldn't *dare*."

"Last chance," I warned.

He laughed. "Even you wouldn't be that stupid, boy." He flung open the gate and barged inside.

Really? I thought. *Who's stupid now?*

Keeley hefted his cosh higher and marched straight for me, Rollins following fast at his heels.

I stood my ground and smiled my most terrible smile. Years of abuse at their hands came flooding into my mind. It was one of those moments where I knew my life was going to change forever if I went ahead and did the forbidden.

"Both you bastards have hurt me enough in the past," I said calmly. "Now it's my turn. See how you like this." I unclipped both leashes at once, and the dogs shot straight at them.

The men had no chance. The expressions on their faces were pretty comical really, almost cartoonish, as they skidded to a halt and spun on their heels. Each tried to shove past the other to avoid being left behind. Major leapt up and grabbed Keeley's shoulder. He screamed and tried to bolt through the gate but misjudged it. He bounced off a post, with Major's teeth still buried in his shoulder. Squeezing through at last, he dragged the huge dog with him. Meanwhile Rex had grabbed Rollins by the leg, and the man squealed like a pig being slaughtered. Rex only tightened his hold and shook his big, shaggy head like he was shaking a rat, sinking his teeth in even deeper.

Somehow both men made it to the Fiat, yanked open the doors, and threw themselves inside, slamming the doors shut behind them.

"Back!" I shouted. "Major! Rex! Heel!"

Reluctantly the dogs padded back to me, both panting heavily. I placed a hand on each dog's head and the three of us stood there, looking at the teachers trapped inside the car. Their wide-eyed faces stared out the windows at us.

My heart was hammering away in my chest but I felt good. For the first time in my school career those sadistic bastards hadn't been able to simply flog me as much as they wanted. I'd finally triumphed against them. What a victory! But then I glanced up the street and saw Mammy pedaling home on her bike. I froze.

She dismounted as both bastard teachers got out of the car and started shouting at her.

I hadn't eaten all day, and now I'd used up all my energy. I sank to the ground, wondering muzzily if those two sadistic bastards would flog me in front of Mammy. If they did, I wouldn't be able to protect myself now.

Mammy made me go back to school the next day. I didn't want to go, of course, but Dad left me no choice. That night I'd been belted harder than I thought possible and was banished to the coal shed again. Now so sore and exhausted, I felt completely detached from everything and everyone.

What could those teachers do to me anyway when I returned to school? They could flog me raw, but they couldn't erase the memory of me setting the dogs on them. I'd fought back and that was victory enough.

Keeley and Rollins were at school wearing bandages. I was surprised by their quietness. They glared, but otherwise ignored me. There was no more talk about repeating kindergarten. Mammy must have made an official complaint against them.

Despite my small victory, I retreated into myself even more, tuning everyone out—even my brothers. I might have won the battle, but I certainly hadn't won the war. Life was still terrible inside that bloody school.

— ~ —

A week later, my brothers and I were walking home for lunch. Side by side, we swung our hurleys, laughing and squabbling as usual. We stopped in shock.

A grey van was parked outside our house and Major and Rex were inside, scrabbling at the metal walls, barking their heads off. It was the dog warden.

"Stop!" we screamed racing towards the van. Hearing us, the dogs' went manic, their paws clawing harder, their barking getting frenetic. But before we could reach it, the van slowly pulled away from the curb.

We were desperate and ran as fast as we could until we were running alongside the driver's window. "Let our dogs go!" we screamed at the man. Maybe he'd stop if he understood how much we loved them. He stared at us through his window before accelerating.

We ran harder and shouted our hearts out as we chased after the van, hammering on the back doors with our hurley sticks. The dogs became even more hysterical. It tore my heart listening to them trying to scratch their way out through the metal.

The van sped up and soon was gone. I stood in the middle of our road, staring after it.

John and Andrew bolted inside to ask Mammy what was happening, but I already knew. Rex and Major were going to be euthanized for attacking my teachers, and it was all my fault. This was Keeley, Rollins, and Crowe getting their revenge.

I somehow managed to drag myself inside. Mammy was in the kitchen crying. John and Andrew wouldn't look at me. Tears were running down their cheeks.

My heart was pounding wildly. "Are they going to be put down?"

Mammy lifted her eyes to me. They were red from crying. "Yes. The warden had a council order for their destruction for being dangerous dogs," she said quietly. She looked away.

My heart was shriveling from guilt. There was only one reason those magnificent dogs were on their way to be killed: me. Charlie Clarke's words came back to me. "The problem with most people when it comes to animals, is they don't think of the consequences." It was like I was murdering Major and Rex with my own hands. Andrew and John couldn't look at me. I'd never felt more alone in my life—or hated myself more.

<center>~~~</center>

Mammy was adamant. "You have to go back to class this afternoon, Marcine. Show the teachers you won't be defeated." I was too devastated to argue.

Keeley was gleefully awaiting my return. Looking straight at me, he clapped his hands to get everyone's attention. "Now class," he said, suddenly pretending to be very somber. "I'd like us all to give a minute's silence for the Fauls' dogs, please."

Numb, I watched him bow his head mockingly like he was respectfully honoring the dead. He stood there for a few minutes, his eyes peacefully closed, an evil smile on his face. He was enjoying every second of his revenge.

The class tittered. Some even mimicked him, bowing their heads, smirking. Andrew, John, and I could only look at Keeley with complete loathing.

In honor of Major and Rex, we sought our revenge right after school. We were waiting for Keeley as he pulled out of the teachers' parking lot. There he was, smirking at us through his windshield.

"Enjoy this instead, you evil bastard," I murmured. We decided to give him a taste of how terrified Major and Rex must have felt inside the warden's van.

"Let's go," said Andrew. We stepped out in front of his car. Keeley skidded to a halt. Panicking, he quickly rolled up his windows, locked the doors, and stared at us in horror.

We raised our hurley sticks and started bashing his car as hard as we could. The noise was horrific. Our sticks banged against the metal like gunshots.

"This is for killing our dogs!" I screamed.

"Come on!" yelled Andrew. "Use our hurleys to tip him over." We jammed our sticks under the car, trying to use them as levers.

Of course, the car was too heavy. Frustrated, we started leaning against the car instead, rocking it hard from side to side. The little car creaked and groaned as it tipped in each direction. Inside Keeley was white with terror. We nearly had it over when we heard a shout.

"What the Hell's going on here?" It was Headmaster Crowe, storming out to see what the commotion was about.

We may not have been able to save poor Major and Rex, but at least we'd taught that sadistic bully a lesson. You could mock us, but not the dogs we'd loved and respected so much.

As for Major and Rex, nothing could erase my guilt about their deaths. I'd asked them to fight my battles for me. I should have realized how much danger I was putting them in. I'd been selfish. Worse, I'd been a coward instead of a true Celtic warrior.

CHAPTER 14

Sterner Stuff

NOT A DAY WENT BY THAT I DIDN'T THINK ABOUT MAJOR and Rex and what had happened to them, but my new family of dogs constantly kept me on my toes. We were also about to get a new addition. Skitty was a new dog who moved in to the barn with a bang.

The day started ordinary enough. We were all lying around the hay in Joe Duffy's barn listlessly. We'd moved in here almost a year ago after we finally outstayed our welcome at poor Padraig's. Joe was another quiet Garryowen bachelor farmer, and luckily for me, he seemed half deaf too. The dogs and I were looking at another endless afternoon stretching out ahead of us. Outside the rain was hammering down on the roof.

"I'm so bored, bored, *bored!*" I yelled at the top of my lungs. "Let's go run around in the rain?" I suggested hopefully.

Lightning flashed, thunder rolled nearby.

The dogs lowered their ears and slouched lower in the hay as if to say, *No, thanks.*

The next minute, a bedraggled mongrel we'd never seen before slunk up the haystack and bolted past us for the far corner. We all watched, our mouths open in shock. "Wuff!" barked Mossy in astonishment. The strange dog shook itself, then lay down behind a pile of hay out of sight. Suddenly, my dogs tore after the newcomer, outraged at being caught off-guard.

"Leave it!" I yelled. There was wild yelping and vicious barking until at last I got them apart. I sat back in the hay, holding Mossy tight in my arms. He wriggled, determined to show this uninvited gatecrasher who was top dog. "Enough!" I snapped. "Leave it."

Mossy stopped struggling and went quiet.

I looked at the new dog cowering in the corner and my heart went out to her. She was some sort of whippet mix shivering all over. Skinny, hungry, and with big, terrified eyes.

Lightning flashed again and thunder rolled low overhead like a giant wooden ball rolling across the sky. Our candle flickered but stayed lit.

I called my dogs to me. "Come on. If we leave her alone, she might relax a little," I said. "Maybe she'll come over when she's ready." I walked back to where we'd been, sat down and relaxed, and yawned until my dogs started lying down around me in a circle.

"Let me tell you a story," I said. "About how a warrior boy called Finn Mac Cool got great wisdom from cooking a magical salmon."

The dogs lay down with their chins on their paws. Listening to ancient Irish stories always bored them into dozing off.

I glanced over at the new dog and caught a glimpse of her big brown eyes before she ducked down into the hay in terror again.

We barely saw this new dog for three days. She snuck out to scrounge for food when we were asleep and hid the rest of the time among piles of hay in the far corner. Since I ignored her as though she didn't exist, my dogs decided to ignore her too. And because my point score was much higher than theirs, they followed my wishes. If I saw her brown eyes peeping over the hay at me, I'd slowly yawn and sleepily closed my eyes for a long moment. I wanted to convey to her, *You're safe here with us. Just relax. Take your time.* After the third day, I said in my calmest voice, "You're a shy one, aren't you? I reckon we'll call you Skitty."

Skitty ended up staying and joining our gang, which was unusual. We'd had many new dogs pass through our barns, but most of the time they put strain on everyone. "Bit like having an uninvited guest come and crash on your couch," I grumbled once. We had an extremely annoying mongrel called Billy for two exhausting weeks. He'd definitely overstayed his welcome. He kept trying to sniff Missy in a rude way. He did it once too often, and Red—always the knight in shining armor for his beloved Missy—chased the mannerless Billy out of the barn. We never saw him again. After similar bad experiences, I decided not to let new dogs stay more than a week. Of course, I found them fascinating to watch, but they invariably caused too much stress if they stayed under our roof for too long. "Blackie!" I'd find myself saying repeatedly. "Stop growling. Leave the new dog alone!"

According to the rules of the dog world, any new dog that arrived had to start at the bottom of the pack and socially climb its way up by winning lots of challenges. For us, this meant we had to learn each trick the new dog tossed at us. "Haven't seen that challenge before," I'd often find myself saying as the new dog won vital points off me.

Pleased with its victory, the dog would walk off while the others glared with loathing. I already had enough problems managing six dogs without refereeing any more drama.

Then I'd remember how my triplet brothers and I had squabbled ferociously over absolutely everything. "Yeah, okay, I get it," I'd say with a sigh. "But can't you dogs leave me out of it?" This was impossible. Since I was the leader of the gang, it was my job to sort out any disputes.

Surprisingly, Skitty was made of sterner stuff than I first thought. She might look like the world's puniest coward, but she had a steely stubbornness none of my dogs could break. I soon learned she was a master manipulator and a cheeky little devil! Missy, of course, hated her. She and Skitty, the only females in our gang, were like two great Hollywood divas vying ruthlessly for the limelight.

"Look at you, Skitty," I said to her at one point. "You're winning most of the challenges. Only Mossy and I are beating you now." One thing she taught me was what good actors dogs could be. Being around her I learned how to read the energy coming off dogs. It was the only way to tell if she was lying about being scared or not. Energy always tells the truth.

The other dogs had a way of discovering the truth from her: They could smell it. Since my human nose lacked their keen sense of smell, I had to pretend. "Hmmm, are you challenging me, darlin'?" I'd bend over and sharply sniff the air near her tail. Knowing that I was trying to smell her real feelings, she'd quickly jam her tail between her legs to stop the truth from coming out. She was faking fear to win lots of points. "Ha!" I'd say. "You weren't scared, you liar. You're just faking it."

❧

I became extremely gifted at reading the energy of any dog I met. Even more amazing was that I learned to read human energy, too. It was like discovering I now had the best warrior armor protecting me. At last I had the confidence to begin seeking out kids my own age again.

"Hi, how's it going?" I'd say shyly to any kind-looking boy I met in Garryowen. Most said "hi" back and started chatting. Meeting kids through my coal delivery job was no problem because I always felt safe with Brandon at my side. It was the local kids I was most wary of—the ones I didn't know except by sight. I'd been teased too often and without provocation. However, now that I could read human energy well, I could relax a bit.

I gradually made more friends. The other members of my hurling team had always been very welcoming and there were other nice kids around the neighborhood. Brandon made a real effort to introduce me to his friends from his school.

However, it remained pretty daunting for me to meet anyone new. The longer I spent away from people, the more I *wanted* to stay away. Being a hermit was like a drug and my privacy had become addictive. It took the suicide of a local boy for me to realize I had to drastically change my life. The poor bastard had taken a gas camper bottle with a hose coming out of it, tied a plastic bag over his head, and laid down in a field, breathing in the noxious gas until he died.

Not long after that, another very depressed and troubled boy died sniffing glue. He passed out while sniffing the bag and when it stuck to his face, he suffocated.

When I found out about both these deaths, I sat with the dogs in the barn, shivering and wrapping my arms tight around my knees. I'd known both boys. "Oh Jesus," I said over and over again. "Am I going to die like that? Alone in one of these barns with you lot hanging around 'til someone discovers my body?" Smelling my fear and sadness, the dogs licked my face as if to reassure me, *You're okay, Martin. You're safe here with us. Don't worry.*

I rubbed their ears in gratitude while I shuddered in shock. "Oh God, oh God. What might have happened to me if I hadn't met you dogs?" Deep down I knew I could have easily committed suicide or sniffed glue or taken up drugs. These wonderful dogs had saved me from all those nightmare scenarios. But the real reason I couldn't shake my fear was because I couldn't see any sort of a future for me. I had no education. No skills. No talent. I was just a feral street kid, and the only thing keeping my mind, heart, and soul together were these six stray dogs. "If you can see a nice future for me, now would be the time to share it," I said grimly to them.

Desperate for some adult human advice, I sought out Sean Fitz, a merchant seaman who'd retired to Garryowen after a lifetime of travelling the world. I'd met him recently through Brandon and he was always patient enough to listen.

"Geez, Sean, what's going to happen to me? I keep dreaming I'm going to end up in some barn dead and no one'll know for weeks." I was fidgeting with the sleeve of my sweater. "I can't see a way out."

Sean was a kind, wise old fellow. "Never feel like you're trapped forever in a horrible situation you can't change, Martin." He puffed on his cigarette and lit one for me. "You're just different from people around here. Not worse—just different. You'll find a place somewhere in the world that understands you better. It just won't be around here. Don't panic," he said. "Leave Garryowen when it feels right. Go see what else the rest of the world has to offer."

I knew instinctively it was the right advice for me. I now had some sort of rough plan for the future. One day I'd leave and travel to another country to start a new life, but what on earth was I going to do about the dogs?

∽

Disaster struck a month later when Fergus went missing.

The first two days he was gone, I tried to ignore that niggling voice inside my head. He was often going off by himself to hunt rats and wild rabbits. "He'll be back again like he always is," I said to the dogs, trying to reassure myself.

They kept restlessly staring out the door of the barn.

By the third day, I was desperately worried. "I'm going to look for him," I said. "Can't stand this waiting one minute more."

Since it was pouring, the dogs refused to step outside and get wet, so I tramped along the railway line getting soaked. I checked around all the ditches, fields, and the hedges. I searched the entire district.

Finally I stumbled upon his body in a field. The rain had washed him spotlessly clean but he'd obviously been shot by a farmer's double-barreled shotgun. His white body was spread out in the grass, peppered with black holes. His hair was clean but strangely flattened. It was an eerie sensation seeing him so lifeless. My heart started to break as it finally sank in.

He was dead.

"Oh, Jesus no, Fergus." I fell down on my knees next to him and bit my bottom lip hard, trying my hardest not to cry. This amazing little dog gone! I ran my trembling fingers along his cheek and down his long, comical muzzle covered in white, wiry fuzz. "Need you to come back," I said, rubbing my eyes angrily. Why did an animal as happy and cheerful as Fergus have to die?

Devastated, I buried his body along the railway line under some bushes and put a small cairn of stones over the spot. Afterwards, I stumbled back to the hay barn, unable to stop crying. The dogs gathered around me, pushing and shoving each other aside to smell the scent of death and grief.

"You made me laugh so much," I muttered into the hay mourning the sweet dog who had been curious about everything. When I sat up, I saw that the other dogs had started playing a game of tag. They were wrestling with each other gleefully. Didn't they care that Fergus was dead? I assumed they'd be sad, but their attitude seemed to be *life goes on.* "How kind of you all," I said sarcastically. "Is this how you'd be if I died?" It was a sobering thought.

Days later, I still couldn't throw off my sadness and shock. The dogs were acting as though nothing abnormal had happened, and I felt so utterly betrayed. One of our gang was dead! Was I the only one in the world thinking about him?

"I need to see Mammy" were the words that popped out of my mouth. I think it was the first time I'd ever said them out loud before. There was only one thing I could do. The next day I'd have to sneak home while Mammy was alone in the house. I desperately needed to see her, and feel her comfort and warmth. She'd understand how important Fergus had been to me.

It was surreal walking down the path to our house. When she opened the door, Mammy's eyes went wide with shock. Suddenly shy, I had no idea what to say. There was a whimper and I looked down in surprise. Two young German Shepherds bumped around her legs. They were gorgeous with huge paws and oversized, floppy wolf ears.

"Oh! They're magnificent! Who are they?" I asked, dropping to a knee, fondling them.

"Captain and Major," she said. "Your father got them for me."

The mention of Major brought an unwelcome surge of guilt. The memory was still too sad and raw.

I saw how nervous she was, so I awkwardly reached out to hug her. We both felt like strangers; neither of us knew how to act or what to say.

Mammy broke the silence. "Marcine, it's so good to see you here. Thank you for coming to see me." She leaned in again, kissed my cheek shyly and led me inside.

We sat on opposite ends of the couch and simply stared at each other.

"Are you home for good now, Marcine?" she whispered at last.

I wished I could tell her what she wanted to hear but I didn't want to lie. There was no way I was coming home.

"One of my dogs died," I said and took a deep breath. "His name was Fergus. He was . . . such a good dog. I miss him." I paused to catch my breath. "You see the other dogs don't care at all that he's gone. I wanted to come and see you. Needed to."

She looked at me kindly and nodded as she patted the couch next to her. "Come. Sit with me. Together we'll watch TV while my favorite show is on. That will relax us and then we can talk."

We sat together and I stared at the screen, but all the while I was really absorbing her presence. Her familiar smell. The French cologne I knew from sniffing the tiny bottle on her dressing table years ago. Her calm, steady energy. Her warmth. Mammy.

She was truly the bedrock of our family. The glue that kept the household functioning. The blonde, Nordic-looking princess who'd ended up living a life very different from what she'd probably dreamt for herself. She was an incredible woman, and I admired her so much.

When her TV show was over, she switched it off and happily turned to me. The show had been like a shot of adrenaline to her body, and the sparkle was back in her blue eyes. For once there weren't any kids destroying her peace, and we had time to talk. It was another precious moment we'd grabbed together, like the evening I watched her bake the Black Forest Cake.

"Can I tell you a bit about Fergus?" I asked.

"Yes, Marcine. Tell me."

After I finished she hugged me tight, and her hug nearly undid me. How could I stay strong and independent while she held me like that? At last I pulled away, rubbing my eyes ferociously.

She wiped away her own tears. "I've been talking to doctors about your hyperactivity," she said quietly. "I understand how difficult school must have been for you," she said. Then she told me she didn't feel so exhausted these days because the kids were older and more independent, and that Dad was now going to AA meetings.

"He's stopped drinking."

So it was true. I'd heard rumors.

"He's a good man now," she said. "He should never drink. It's not him when he drinks. . . . Will you come home now?"

My heart melted before her quiet, pleading eyes. "Maybe," I said, reaching out and holding her hand. "Soon, but not yet." I had so many questions that needed answering before I moved back home. Could I give up my freedom and independence?

Could I even live under the same roof with so many humans? More importantly, what would I do with all my dogs?

"Sorry, Mammy," I spoke into her shoulder as I hugged her goodbye. Guilt was gnawing at my guts like a rat. "I'll think about moving back home soon. I promise. Just give me some time."

Deep down I knew I still needed my six dogs too much, and they certainly needed me. However, the visit had been a good thing. As I walked back to my barn, my footsteps felt lighter than usual. The door at home was open if I wanted to return. The question was, could I really live with humans again?

CHAPTER 15

Getting Wilder

BACK WHEN I WAS STILL AT HOME, I KNEW THAT I WAS GETTING wilder. I couldn't help it. After Major and Rex had been put down for protecting me from Mr. Crowe and Mr. Keeley, my life just wasn't the same. My family was being pushed beyond endurance by my insolence, but I couldn't help myself. I was so unhappy.

One morning I was alone, slipping through the back lanes of Garryowen, when a boy stepped out in front of me.

"Hi ya, freak," he said. My heart sank. It was Nane, one of the three bully boys who'd painted the swastika on our house. He smiled, becoming even uglier than usual. "You still look like a scrawny little loser, don't you?" he sneered.

I looked him in the eye. There was no way I wasn't fighting back. "Scrawny, huh? Didn't stop me from giving you a good flogging last time I saw you," I said calmly. I heard a noise behind me and spun around. It was his friend, Ger, looking even uglier. They laughed together, and the hairs went up on the back of my neck. Both boys were a few years older than I was and definitely bigger and stronger. I wondered where their leader Malarky was.

Then there was an explosion of pain right to my kidneys. I doubled over and felt my arms twisted behind my back so I couldn't move. I looked straight up into the sparkling eyes of Malarky. I'd never seen him more overjoyed.

He laughed and spat in my face. "Hello, Faullie. I've been wantin' a chat with you."

Nane and Ger twisted my arms harder until I was afraid they'd snap my bones.

I was really scared now, but there was no way I was letting Malarky see that. Besides, how much worse could they beat me than my teachers and Dad already had? There wasn't much of a beating I couldn't take these days.

Malarky looked at Nane. "You check if he's the right one?"

"Yeah, that's him. He's got that freaky white patch of hair on the back of his head. He's the fucker that smashed you."

Malarky smiled in a way that made my skin crawl; his eyes were scary-weird. The calmer he got, the creepier he became. He lit a cigarette and blew the smoke in my face. "Want to know a funny story, Faullie? Once upon a time there were three little freaks, and their daddy was Adolf Hitler."

Ger and Nane laughed.

"These three skinny freaks were born in Ireland and annoyed all the other kids. One day the world decided it would be a better place if one of them kind of . . ." he paused, shrugging, "died."

I nervously watched him walk over to the fence where some rope lay on the ground. He picked it up so I could see there was a noose knotted at one end.

"Yeah," he continued. "It's a story with an unhappy ending. To start with there were three little Faullies and then there were . . . two."

I fought as hard as I could to break free, but I wasn't strong enough. It was as simple as that.

The three boys dragged me standing through a nearby backyard gate, then as soon as I was inside, they tripped me so I was sprawled face down on the ground. Then they started dragging me again. I could feel myself starting to go numb with shock. I couldn't possibly be about to die. I was somewhere in a backyard in Garryowen. This wasn't real. Within seconds the shock passed. This was real alright. In my soul I made a decision. I certainly wasn't going to make this easy for them. If I was going to die then I wasn't going to die a coward.

The loop of rope came over my head and was yanked tighter. I was being dragged towards a tree in the middle of the backyard. No one was laughing now. All I heard were grunts as they kept hauling me. The rope around my neck was getting tighter. My lungs were gulping for air, and my eyeballs were bulging from their sockets.

Nane and Ger held me still while they waited for Malarky to throw the end of the rope over one of tree branches.

"That's it," he panted hoarsely. "Bring him closer underneath." They dragged me closer and then hoisted me to my feet.

"Pull!" screamed Malarky.

The rope suddenly burned like fire around my neck. They heaved again. My feet left the ground, and I nearly fainted. My neck felt like it was about to snap.

"Let's go!" yelled Malarky. "Leave the freak. Run!"

I swung around in a slow, suspended circle. *I am hanging by my neck from a tree,* I said to myself. The thought was crazy, but the pain was agonizingly real.

No one was there to save me. My fingers frantically clutched and clawed at the rope, but my body was pulling me down too much. I reached upwards and felt the underside of the branch with my fingertips. I stretched out my arm and grasped at the air. Somehow, unbelievably, my fingers found their hold and I managed to pull myself up. As soon as I had the energy, I loosened the rope from around my neck and took in breath after precious breath of air. Then I threw the rope off like it was a poisonous snake.

After a while, I staggered home. I curled up in a ball on the bed and trembled and shook for hours.

Andrew and John came home and were horrified when they saw my neck so raw and inflamed. It was obvious someone had tried to hang me. Panicking, they ran and told Mammy but even though she begged me, I refused to say who'd done it.

She called the police, but I still wouldn't tell anyone. I knew if Andrew and John discovered their names they'd go right out to fight Malarky, Ger, and Nane. God only knew what they'd do. I cared about my brothers' safety much more than revenge.

—◆—

Things got even worse when I stole the rent money out of Mammy's purse.

I found her at the kitchen table rocking back and forth, staring into her empty purse. "Oh my God, vat am I going to do?" I'd never seen her this upset. Her face was white with fright. I looked on as shame writhed in my gut.

"You took the money, didn't you?" she asked, not turning her head towards me.

I shifted uneasily from foot to foot. "Hey, Dad takes money out of your purse all the time," I said sullenly. "Then he drinks it all. You must be used to it by now. Anyway, you always find a way of paying the rent."

I glanced at her and saw the crushing sense of helplessness enveloping her. The worst part was I couldn't give the money back because I'd already spent it. All day I'd been feeling like a big man buying chocolate bars, packs of cigarettes, and bottles of cider for all the boys I knew around the neighborhood. I'd even given some of them cash. I was trying to buy their friendship, but it hadn't worked. They'd taken the things from me, then laughed in my face. "Thanks, Faul, but we still don't like you. Don't you get it? You're a dumb freak. Nobody's ever going to like you." It had been one of the most pathetic things I'd ever done. Now it was time to face the music.

Mammy kept staring into her empty purse. Her silence was much worse than her screaming. She wouldn't even look at me. She quietly clicked her purse shut. "Go to your room. Wait there."

Dad came home from work. I heard the two of them talk quietly in the kitchen, then heard his heavy footsteps on the stairs. For once I knew I deserved this punishment.

Afterwards, I crawled into bed, exhausted from crying. I heard muffled sounds of my family sitting down to dinner. I already knew that when Dad finished his meal, he was coming to take me to the coal shed. I hated the place even more now Major and Rex were gone.

Through my tears, I looked numbly at the bedroom wall and saw all the scuff marks left by our shoes when John, Andrew, and I wrestled together. I'd always thought the marks looked a bit like a map of the world. Over the years I'd stared at that map, dreaming of all the exotic places I could escape to.

Shit, why am I still bothering to live here? The thought slipped into my mind without warning. Straight away, it was joined by another. *Why not run away?* The breath caught in my throat. It wasn't such a crazy idea, was it? Surely anywhere would be better than living here. What did I have to look forward to? More hell at school, more unhappiness at home, more nights in the coal shed, and more floggings. I couldn't see how things could ever improve.

I knew I was driving poor Mammy crazy because I couldn't stop acting out and doing stupid things. She'd be better off without me in her life. But could I really just run away? *Yep. I can even leave right now if I want to.*

I could hear my family downstairs eating, talking, and laughing. The only times they sounded that relaxed was when I wasn't around. Truth was, the whole family would be better off without me.

Okay. Time to do something about it. I took a deep, shuddering breath, and, as though in a dream, I walked slowly towards the window and climbed onto the ledge. *Look at me. Here I am running away from home.* I shimmied down the drainpipe, walked up our front path, and out the gate.

I'm never going back again, I swore to myself. *Humans can get stuffed. I've had enough.* From now on I was going to live on my own terms, no matter what the price.

CHAPTER 16

Joining the Human World Again

EVERY TIME I VENTURED OUT INTO THE HUMAN WORLD again, like playing in hurling matches with the Saints on Sundays, was starting to feel like a holiday from the dogs. For a few precious hours I could throw off all my responsibilities of being in charge of them and just play the game I loved.

When we won what turned out to be an electrifying draw against Monaleen, I was elated.

"Brilliant! Well played! Join us for a drink, Martin?" asked my brother John.

"Of course," I panted, jogging beside him. "We'll have a great *craic*." Yet while I listened to him talking about the game, I couldn't stop thinking of the dogs.

I felt my stomach churn from nerves. Would the farmer come looking for them with his shot gun? We were now living in Tom Clancy's hay barn, and since he wasn't deaf like Padraig and Joe Duffy, I worried about the dogs barking when they were left on their own. They were fine during the day, but the later I stayed out at night, the more they worried—and barked.

My conscience poked at me hard. I should go home rather than stay for a drink with the team. *Think about what happened to poor Fergus*, I advised myself. *You don't want Tom shooting the dogs.*

"Martin! Over here! Share this with us!" It was the captain of the team, raising a bottle of cider in the air.

Fuck it. "Coming!" I yelled and jogged over, shrugging off my guilt. I was getting so sick of worrying about the dogs all the time. They were beginning to feel like six albatrosses around my neck. Cruel, but true. Why did I feel so guilty just because I wanted to make some human friends?

The team greeted me with a rousing cheer. "Excellent, Martin! Have a seat. What a great game, eh? Want a drink?"

"Yeah, thanks," I said cheerfully, accepting the bottle. I took a swig and then passed it on to the teammate sitting next to me. Laughter and talk flowed around me and I loved it. Dogs be damned, it was time to enjoy myself.

We sat around celebrating for hours, passing around the bottle and then another, all the while swapping stories and having a great *craic*. I was in heaven. I was just about to tell another funny story when the boy beside me stood up.

"Ah well, that's it for me, boys," he said. "School tomorrow and it's getting late."

Everyone else started standing up too and gathering their things.

I sat bolt upright and looked around in shock. "Hey! Where's everyone going? I thought we were having fun." I felt all my old panic return. *Why am I being left behind again?*

"Sorry, Faullie. Bit tired. Was a great game. See you next week at training, eh?" the team captain said.

Watching the other boys walk away, the truth hit me like a cold slap in the face. The rest of the team had homes to return to and I didn't. Suddenly the hay barn and the dogs didn't seem enough. I quickly arranged a smile on my face and replied, "Yeah, no problem. See you at training next week. Bye."

"I don't want to go back to the barn," I suddenly said aloud after they'd left. Trudging reluctantly to Tom Clancy's barn, I gave myself a stern talking-to. "What the hell are you whining about, Martin? You love the dogs. They're your family now. And the barn's not so bad." As I crawled through Tom's hedge, heading across the field in the moonlight, a voice inside me said, *Be honest. The dogs are beginning to bore you.*

My stomach started churning again. On the one hand, I felt like I was betraying the dogs in the worst possible way. On the other, I couldn't stop thinking of all the things I was missing out on because of them.

The cows were lying down in the field, their big sleek backs shiny in the moonlight. "It's okay, girls," I murmured as I passed. "Only me." I'd come through these fields so many times, they knew me well.

Tonight had been a sharp reminder of how much fun humans could be. What I missed most in my life was having interesting, intelligent human conversation about everything from history to politics. I wanted to share funny stories and jokes with boys my own age. I wanted to meet girls.

By the time I reached the barn I was extremely restless and irritable, like I didn't quite fit in my own skin any more. As I climbed the wall struts to the loft, my frustration rose with every step. I looked around as I lit the usual forbidden candle. "Shit, this place is a dump."

The dogs came rushing out of the hay to greet me. I looked at them sullenly as they swarmed around me, jumping up, licking me, and nudging me for pats.

"Yeah, great," I muttered. "Just what I'm in the mood for." Once upon a time I would have thought the dogs were being wonderfully affectionate. Now I knew better. "*Aaaagh!* Why are you dogs so obsessed about your stupid game? Who *cares* about who's in charge! Leave me alone for once!" I snapped. I barged past them and sulkily sat down in the hay with my back against the wall folding my arms. They wouldn't stop pestering me, so I lifted my chin, turned my head away, and yawned. In other words, *It's okay. I'm still in charge. I'm calm now and nothing's wrong. Go away and relax. No need to keep testing me.*

All of them laid down, but each dog kept a wary eye on me.

I pulled a layer of thick hay over myself and shut my eyes tight. With a sigh, I opened them again. Poor dogs, I was the center of their universe. They hated it when I was angry or tense. I yawned loudly and blew out the candle. "Go to sleep now. I'll be fine in the morning." Their tails wagged in the hay. I had to face the truth. I was surrounded by dogs who loved me, but for the first time their love felt suffocating.

In my new mood of restlessness, I went to Brendan Mullins's slaughterhouse to feed the dogs the next night. As I stood handing out the chunks of stinking meat outside the fence, I considered the evening's options. *Well, Martin, you can return to that bloody barn with the dogs and go crazy with boredom or you can go stay at a friend's house.* It was beginning to dawn on me that I had options; I could do whatever the hell I wanted! I threw the last chunk of meat to Blackie and said, "Sorry dogs, but I'm out of here. Going visiting for once."

Curious, the dogs stayed glued to my heels as I headed down the railway line. I'd already made up my mind where I'd stay that night. I'd recently made friends with the Bourne family, especially with their son, Neil. He'd offered me a couch to sleep on many times, and I finally felt like taking him up on his offer.

I left the dogs on the railway line, sternly ordering them home. I couldn't stop the stupid butterflies flittering about inside my stomach as I walked down into Garryowen.

The Bournes lived in a gracious Edwardian-style house with a fanlight window above the big front door, and a portico flanked by pillars. I'd had no idea it was so nice. "Must be bloody rich," I murmured under my breath.

As I rang the doorbell, I remembered that Neil had told me their family once had money because their father had been a businessman in America. His widow had returned to Garryowen and lived there with her three sons. From our few meetings down the street, I knew the Bournes were true eccentrics. For starters, they were passionate socialists. They thought how I lived with the dogs in the barn was "marvelous." And that my decision to live rough was "a powerful statement against all capitalist pigs."

Personally, I thought they were a bit barmy.

The door swung open wide. "Hell-o, Martin. Please *do* come inside." It was Mrs. Bourne wearing a silk kimono. She held a cigarette holder with an unusually fat hand-rolled cigarette jammed in it in her languid hand. There was a brimming glass of gin in her other hand. As usual, she was utterly charming. "This way, darling. Follow me. The boys are in the drawing room trying to light a fire. Not having much luck I'm afraid." She led me through rooms graciously appointed with high ceilings, beautiful windows swathed in lavish curtains, silk-covered chairs and sofas, and watercolors and lovely oil paintings of landscapes dotting the walls.

I noticed a few odd touches like the poster of Che Guevara above the fireplace. There were others of John Lennon, Martin Luther King, Jr., Jimi Hendrix, and Led Zeppelin scattered about the house.

Everything else looked expensive but shabby. There were swathes of cobwebs hanging from the ceiling corners and chandeliers. On every flat surface were empty bottles of cider and gin glasses. I was used to dirt, of course, but not in a place of such affluence. Mammy would have had an instant heart-attack.

Neil and his brothers John and Rory were huddled around the fireplace. I shivered suddenly because the room was freezing, colder even than it was outside.

Geez. It's warmer in my hay barn, I thought. *So much for enjoying a night of luxury sleeping in a real house.*

The boys looked up with welcoming smiles. "Hello, Martin!" said Neil. "Great to see you! Come and help. The fire's being an utter bastard of a thing."

They had upper-class accents and wore nice clothes, which were a bit shabby like the rest of the house. Neil handed me a bottle of cider.

Now we're talking, I thought happily.

Neil grinned back. "It'll help you stay warm. Maybe you can help? We can't get this fire going at all."

I looked at their pathetic attempt. All they had was one small measly lump of coal. The poor thing was spluttering away, failing to light properly.

"Sorry," laughed Neil, "Charlotte didn't pay the gas bill so they've cut us off." He grinned up at his mother. "Bought your weekly stash of gin and smoke-lolly instead. Didn't you, darling?"

Mrs. Bourne raised the fat cigarette and glass of gin and smiled wolfishly. "When life's so short, live damned hard," she drawled.

It took me a moment to realize Neil was actually calling his mother by her first name. *Charlotte.* Mammy would have clipped me over the ear if I dared address her like that. I looked at the boys, confused. "Er . . . what's smoke-lolly?"

"Marijuana," said Neil over his shoulder as he fiddled with the coal. "We buy it from the bikers in Garryowen."

His brother tossed a paper bag over to me. "Here. Roll yourself one."

I looked down at the bag bewildered. I had no idea what to do. Neil rolled me a joint, then his mother held out her slim gold Dunhill lighter. I thought it couldn't be too bad if Mrs. Bourne was smoking it. I took a few sharp puffs then breathed in deeply.

Ugh! It was like smoking lawn clippings. I grabbed the cider and guzzled it down before I coughed to death. My head swam around muzzily. Did people really do this to relax? The floor tilted weirdly so I collapsed into the nearest chair. Che Guevara reeled above me, smiling down weirdly.

No one else noticed. They were too busy rolling joints as they stared at the lump of coal and made suggestions about how to get it lit. No one could agree.

"I've got the munchies," said Mrs. Bourne decisively. She turned to Rory. "Be a pet, darling, and throw a potato in the pot for dinner."

"Sorry," Rory countered. "No can do. You forgot to pay the gas bill, so no gas."

John blew smoke rings in a thoughtful way. "Here's an idea. Why don't we put the potato *inside* the kettle? Then put the kettle on the embers. Surely it'll cook that way."

Neil shook his head. "No can do. This damned lump of coal won't light, so the kettle won't boil."

I giggled. This family sure loved the phrase, "No can do."

"The problem is," I said, speaking carefully because my lips felt so numb. "You have only *one* piece of coal. You'll need more than that to make a decent fire." The three boys and Mrs. Bourne turned to look at me with respect.

She raised her glass to me. "You are so *profoundly* right, Martin. I hereby declare you to be a true intellectual. Welcome!"

The three boys raised clenched fists in the direction of the poster of Che Guevara. "Well done. Take back the power!"

I had no idea what they were talking about but suddenly felt an intense craving for food. "Do you mind if I grab something to eat?"

Neil smiled happily and punched the air. "You do that, Martin. Take back the power!"

I stumbled into the kitchen and opened the fridge. There was nothing to eat on any of the shelves. Literally nothing. Then I tried every cupboard and all the drawers. There was no food in the house except for three raw potatoes. *This is crazy. Come to think of it, everyone under this roof is bloody crazy.*

I lurched back to the drawing room. "Gotta go home," I mumbled. "Feed my dogs."

The Bourne boys smiled and punched clenched fists into the air, surrounded by clouds of pungent smoke. "Take back the power!"

"You do that, pet," drawled Mrs. Bourne.

Neil looked at me with completely stoned eyes. "That's the way, brother. Don't give in to the machine!"

As I stumbled through the darkening streets of Garryowen, I thought of house I'd just left and the charming, well-mannered, but definitely eccentric Bourne family who lived in it. I wouldn't have survived a single night there. It'd been like watching civilization crumbling very slowly into chaos. My mind started to clear a fraction as the cold night air swirled around me. "Wow, dogs, all is forgiven. I'm not sure I'm ready to live with humans just yet."

—◦—

A few days later I picked up my wages for delivering coal and felt like a treat. "How about we all get some fish and chips?" I asked the dogs. They wagged their tails in excitement. They knew what those words meant.

I was no longer worried about surviving in the real world after seeing the eccentric Bourne family in action. Surely, I couldn't do any worse than they did. Ever since Brandon had found me a job, I knew I could get work and buy food with my wages. I could probably even live with people if I tried.

But what the hell was I going to do with the dogs? I looked at them as we walked swiftly. "Am I going to be manacled to the lot of you until you eventually die off one by one?" I grumbled. They just grinned back at me and waited patiently at the railway bridge while I headed into Garryowen.

I got a huge parcel of fish and chips from the shop and paused to scoff a few down in peace before I returned to the dogs and their greedy, pleading eyes. They could still play me like a violin.

"Mmmm, Mr. Ford, you've really outdone yourself today," I said as I took a bite of one golden chip. I have to say that I felt pretty damned pleased with myself. *Look at you, Martin. Eating delicious food, and all paid for with your own wages.*

A local tramp trudged past, pushing an old wooden cart with bicycle wheels. It was Old Tommy. He wasn't really all that old; he just looked it. He grinned at me and wriggled his bare fingers at me in a wave. They were yellow with tobacco stains and grubby with dirt.

"Evenin', Martin. Enjoyin' your dinner?" he asked cheerfully. "Just off to get mine." He winked. "Out of the trash, back of the shop."

I smiled politely but as soon as he turned the corner, I hurried off, clutching the newspaper parcel to my chest. *Oh God. Was that going to be me?* Was I going to end up Old Marty, the eccentric tramp with his weird pack of mongrels?

Tommy looked happy enough but there were other tramps around Garryowen who didn't look happy at all. They were old bowed men who drank too much and never stopped muttering to themselves. The thought terrified me. It was time I got serious about my future.

<hr />

My best friend Brandon was concerned too. "Come on, Martin. Don't be silly. Weather's starting to get cold again. It's time to move back home," he said one morning.

We were on our way to fetch the cart and Neddy.

I grunted. I usually told him not to bother nagging, but for once I listened. Seeing Old Tommy had shaken me badly.

"Come on," Brandon urged. "You know it's the right thing to do. Your dad's off the drink now. Going to AA meetings."

I grunted again. Word was going around that Mick Faul was still off the drink and back to being his original, charming self.

Brandon clapped me on the back. "I'll shut up, Martin. But this is the truth. You're killing your mother by staying away like this. You've got to go home. And Bobby wants to talk to you," he told me.

Bobby Mack was a man I respected more than anyone else in Garryowen. He'd once been on a hunger strike in support of the Irish cause and been to prison for his beliefs. He was considered a hero in our area. Once he was released, his hunger strike had ended.

I hesitated. I knew that Mammy and he were friends. "Okay," I said reluctantly. "I'll go."

When I went to see him, Bobby's mother, Mrs. Mack, opened the front door and took me through to the living room. "Martin's here, love," she announced to Bobby.

Bobby was watching TV. He looked up at me blinking. He was going blind because of the time he'd spent in prison. His body had never really recovered.

Mrs. Mack showed me to an armchair. "Sit down, Martin, dear. I'll bring you in some tea and sandwiches."

I glanced down at myself. Hell. I was as grubby as a scarecrow, and her armchair was spotless, so I remained standing. I didn't want to mess up her nice furniture. Bobby was looking at me with a gentle smile.

"How's it going, Bobby?"

"Very well, Martin." He certainly didn't look it. He was badly hunched over and his shoulder blades stuck out. You wouldn't believe he was once more than six feet tall. His once thick, brown hair was mousey and sparse. His big, elegant hands were like twisted dead things sitting on the arms of his chair. The only parts of him that still lit up with his old spark were his face and kind, brown eyes.

"That's grand," I said awkwardly. It was always a bit of a shock seeing Bobby.

"Turn the TV off and have a seat, Martin," he said. "Mam doesn't mind a bit of dirt."

I sat down and could feel his lovely calm energy enveloping me, even though part of me wanted to fight it off. I hated the feeling of being tamely steamrollered by everyone into moving back home again. It was hard for me not to fight back at any pushy behavior when I'd been bullied my whole life. "Well," I said jauntily. "I know why you've called me here. Should I stay and look after the dogs, or should I go home? Guess I should respect your opinion, Bobby." To be honest, I was a little upset with him. I'd hoped he'd be more supportive of my stand for independence. I thought he'd understood my need to live rough with the dogs. After all, he'd gone to prison standing up for his own principles.

His brown eyes looked into mine, and with a jolt of surprise, I saw there was still a core of steely strength in him. He leaned forward. He might have seemed weak but he still had plenty of fight in him. "Martin, are you willing to listen to some well-meant advice?"

I jiggled impatiently. "Sure."

"How you're treating your mother is a disgrace. You should be ashamed of yourself because of how worried she's been over you."

I stared down at my feet in shock. I hadn't expected this and was hurt and confused by the judgment in his voice. Suddenly all I wanted to do was get up and run straight out the door.

Before I could bolt, his mother bustled back into the room. She was holding a big silver tray and had obviously gone to a lot of trouble to make a nice morning tea for me. There was a plate of neatly cut triangle sandwiches and a large orange and poppy-seed cake. On the tray was a teapot of fine porcelain, along with linen napkins, two cups, and pretty little plates. "Come on now, Martin. Don't let me down. I've made a little lunch for you. Please stay and eat."

I wasn't that much of a monster, so I pasted a smile on my face and stayed where I was as she bustled around us, pouring out the tea, arranging the food on a little plate for me.

"There! That might keep you going 'til tea time," she said happily.

What else could I say? "Thank you, Mrs. Mack. It all looks lovely." It was impossible not to like her. She treated everyone with respect, no matter who they were. Look at me, for instance. A feral looking street kid dropping bits of hay and dirt all over her best armchair, and she was treating me like the most important guest she'd had all year.

Bobby sipped some tea. "Listen to your conscience, Martin," he said. "How could any pack of dogs possibly be worth more than your mother? Think about it. I mean *really* think about it. They're tough street strays so they'll survive. You can keep walking over to the railway line and feed them while you live at home."

"But . . ."

He held up a finger. "No, Martin. It's time you stopped *talking* about honor and started *acting* honorably instead. At the moment you're just lying to yourself."

I drank my tea sullenly not looking at him. My stomach was in knots. It always was whenever I felt guilty. I knew he was right. For the past three years, if any thought of Mammy slipped into my mind, I simply shoved it straight out again and ignored it. I certainly wasn't proud of how I'd treated her.

Bobby went quiet, allowing me time and space to think. A clock chimed gently on the mantelpiece.

It *was* time that I thought about Mammy. She was a woman in a foreign country with no relatives nearby to help, trying her hardest to bring up eight children and make her marriage work. Seven of her children were completely happy at home. I'd been the only one not to fit in. It was probably because of my ADHD, but that was hardly her fault. As for my father, she'd managed to do something about his legendary drinking too.

When Bobby decided I'd thought about Mammy enough, he poured me more tea. "Martin, you certainly talk about it a lot, but do you *really* want to grow up to be an honorable man?"

I looked at him, hurt. "You know I do."

"Then I think this is one of those moments in your life when you must decide what the truly honorable thing to do is. It's time you grew up. You have to get rid of all those bad habits that risk your honor. Like lying and thieving and breaking your promises. You know what I'm talking about. Does any of that make you feel proud of yourself?"

I tried shutting him out, but Bobby Mack had a way of effortlessly slicing through all my old excuses. "There's another reason I don't want to go home," I reluctantly admitted. "If I go back I'll get bullied. Believe me, Bobby, it was really fucking horrible." It was the first time I'd admitted to anyone other than a dog how hard all that relentless bullying had been to endure. Everyone—even Andrew and John—had always believed my tough attitude made me invincible. I realized there were stupid tears gathering in the corners of my eyes and rubbed at them furiously.

Bobby looked kindly at me. "Ah, bullies. Yes, they'll always be around, no matter where you go." He probably had seen his share in prison. "Do you want to know how you can make bullies completely irrelevant?" he asked.

"Yeah, of course."

"Decide what you'll stand up for and defend to the death. That's the secret. Once you work that out, no one on this planet can bully you, no matter how hard they try. Do you know why?"

"No."

"Because bullies can't stand people who believe so strongly in something they're prepared to die for it. Scares them."

"I don't understand."

"Believe me, Martin, bullies are always drawn to weakness. As soon as they spot things like confusion, shyness, and uncertainty in people, they close in like vultures to feed." He nodded and then continued. "Deep down bullies are the most frightened people in the world. The more of a bully they are, the more terrified they are of people finding out how scared they are inside. Each time they peck at someone and see they've scored a hit, they don't feel so powerless. It's almost like an addiction for them. The more they feed, the more they need."

I thought of all the bullies I'd known and knew he was right.

Bobby looked straight into my eyes. "So start working out what you feel very strongly about, and start standing up for your beliefs." He held up his finger again. "Because *that's* the exciting moment when you stop being a victim and start radiating strength. Don't worry, as soon as they sense your confidence, the bullies will melt away. It's like invisible armor, and it'll only get stronger the older you get."

I believed him. Bobby Mack had experienced far more than I had and from far more brutal people. It was time I did the truly honorable thing and stopped hurting Mammy. I'd find a way of handling the bullies by following Bobby's advice.

I met his gaze and breathed out hard. "Okay," I said quietly. "You've persuaded me. I'll move back home and see how it goes. But will you do me a favor? Let me decide when."

<hr />

That evening I sat up in Tom Clancy's hay loft, looking out the open barn doors and over his fields. Around me, the evening was beautiful and still. A full moon was turning everything silver.

Bobby's words had profoundly moved me. His natural sense of honor was so strong, it was infectious. After speaking with him, I couldn't help wanting to be the best person I could possibly be. "Bobby, you make the word 'honor' actually mean something," I said aloud into the silence. The dogs were lazing in the hay, scratching at an occasional flea.

Dogs are naturally honorable too, I thought. I remembered all the times these dogs had been honorable to me. They were patient when I didn't understand their language, customs, and rules. Yet they'd still cared about me and always tried to make me feel like one of the gang no matter what I did.

I remembered all the times we'd been hungry, cold, and miserable together, and they hadn't complained. Instead, they'd been optimistic and happy to see me every single time I returned, even when I came back empty-handed. "I've been lucky meeting you, haven't I?"

They wagged their tails noisily in the hay. That's all they ever really wanted—for me to be happy. It was humbling.

I thought of poor Major and Rex who'd protected me with their lives, and had been lethally punished for it. I thought of sweet little Fergus who'd always cheered me up when I was sad. Of all the other dogs who'd been so friendly and welcoming to me over the years. *Why are dogs so honorable?*

"You're all so ready to be happy over the smallest things in life, aren't you? A raw bone. A friendly word. A bit of a rub behind the ears. You want so little from me, don't you?"

Something Tige Kelly had said to me once about a man flashed through my mind. "He has a true generosity of spirit," he'd said. Now I understood what he meant. Dogs have such a natural generosity of spirit. They'd given so much of themselves—all day, every day—ever since I'd known them. When I was around dogs I could truly be myself, and they generously gave me whatever they could—affection, attention, protection, and a sense of belonging. All for so little in return.

There was no way I'd be the same person if I'd been living in these hay barns with six boys, instead of six dogs. That realization said it all really.

Dogs had taught me to be honorable around them. I didn't steal from them. Or trick them. Or tease them. Or bully them. Or lie to them. I was proud of who I was when I was around them. I admired myself for the many sacrifices I'd made for them.

Now Bobby Mack was saying it was time I showed the same honor to the people who mattered in my life. I knew I had no choice, not if I wanted to like myself.

"Okay, Martin. You heard Bobby. You know what you've got to do: Move home for Mammy's sake." My heart started beating faster. *Shit, I don't believe it. I'm actually going home.*

The dogs were oblivious to how I was feeling. I'd never seen them so relaxed and content. "But God knows how I'm going to walk away and leave you all behind," I murmured under my breath.

Brandon came the next day. He sat next to me in the hay and rubbed the dogs' ears as they wandered over to greet him. "Come on, Martin. No point putting it off any longer. Bobby told me he talked to you yesterday. I've come to bring you home."

I nodded. "I need to take the dogs for one last walk," I managed to say. There were tears at the back of my eyes. I was so sad, like a big hole was growing inside me, opening wider with every breath. I stumbled to my feet.

"You okay?" asked Brandon.

I nodded numbly. Sensing something unusual was up, the dogs ran over to me. They sniffed the air around me delicately, trying to make out what was happening. Their ears, chins, and tails sank lower as their eyes searched my face anxiously. I turned to Brandon. "Meet you at the scout hall in a few hours. I want some time to say goodbye to them."

"Sure," he said quietly. He understood how much these dogs meant to me.

Feeling like a traitor, I rubbed them reassuringly behind the ears. "Come on, dogs. Let's go for a walk." How many times had I said that? Now I felt like a lying Judas.

Should we take one last slide down the haystack together? Why not? I pushed off and slid down fast then turned to see the dogs sliding after me, comical as ever. As my feet hit the ground, I felt more tears gathering but I didn't want to cry. I wasn't a baby anymore.

I already knew where I wanted us to go: along the railway line as far away from Garryowen as we could.

"Come on!" I said, half laughing, rubbing fiercely at my eyes. "I want to make this walk really fun." The dogs fanned out either side of me, happy I wasn't acting so strange any more. We walked for at least two hours and I made it the best sort of walk, throwing them sticks, encouraging them to chase rabbits and show off to their heart's content.

They were the most magnificent friends any boy could hope to have.

Pa.

Red.

Blackie.

Missy.

Skitty.

The space that would have been filled by Fergus, were he still with us.

And of course, the first dog to adopt me—funny, bossy Mossy.

I realized how much they'd changed me. When I first met them I was as jumpy as a rabbit. A scowling, angry, defensive kid who thought he was a freak. Worse, a kid who felt like the most stupid boy in the world.

Yet this special gang of dogs had saved me. They'd taught me how to communicate better. Be calmer. More responsible. Had helped me discover peace, honesty, confidence, and trust.

I took a deep breath. "Come on. Time to head back now." Reluctantly, I started walking back towards Garryowen. The dogs wheeled around, racing to catch up with me. Suddenly I knew how to show my thanks in a way they could understand—by making this last lap of the walk especially fun.

"Let's run!" I yelled. They barked in excitement as they galloped after me. Gratitude surged through me. Because of these dogs my life would never be the same again. I was now Martin, the boy who talked to dogs.

We ran until I could see the railway bridge up ahead, which was their territory boundary and the point beyond which they couldn't go. I swallowed hard as my feet slowed to a stop. "Dogs, over here," I called to them. They skidded to a halt and looked back at me, with their tongues lolling out.

I crouched down and patted the ground. I felt the tears coming and bit my bottom lip hard. This was it. Time to say goodbye. "Hi ya, Mossy. Good boy. Hello, Missy, Pa, Red, Skitty. Yeah, you too, Blackie. Come here. There's something I want to tell you all." I sat down on the metal track and let them lick my eyes and cheeks as I cried.

I was leaving the Dirty Dog Gang behind. It was the hardest thing I've ever had to do. I did my best to explain but it was impossible. Their language simply didn't have the words for how I felt.

Brandon was waiting patiently in the shed behind the scout hall. He patted me on the shoulder when I finally appeared.

I couldn't stop the tears that kept coming. Of course, I'd be back along the railway every day to feed the dogs and make sure they were okay, but it wouldn't be the same as living with them.

"Come over here," said Brandon kindly. "You'll have to wash before you go home, Martin." He turned on a tap at the sink. "Better clean yourself up a bit for your Mam. Look. I've brought you soap and a towel." He grinned, trying to cheer me up. "You smell a bit like a wild animal. When was the last time you looked in a mirror?"

I couldn't remember. Nor did I care. I was too busy being numb with misery thinking about the dogs.

Brandon pulled out some scissors. "At least let me cut your hair."

It was past my shoulders and badly matted. Bits of twigs, hay, mud, and tiny pieces of torn blanket were scattered through it. I looked worse than a mongrel dog. But I shook my head no. Keeping my hair was going to be my last precious finger-hold on feeling independent and a reminder of how I'd changed and taken charge of my own destiny. "The hair stays," I said.

Brandon shrugged. "Fine. Look like a feral hick. What do I care?" He helped me wash up a bit then clapped me on the shoulder. "Right, that's the best I can do. At least your mam might recognize you now." He gave me a hug. "Off you go and don't let me down by ducking back to the dogs."

I took a deep breath and started walking home. I should have been nervous but I wasn't. This time everything felt different. I was now ready to face anything the world wanted to throw at me. Bullying, aggression, cruelty, abuse—none of these things scared me anymore. As long as I kept my honor and integrity, I knew my spirit would remain indestructible.

The dogs of Garryowen had taught me well.

I ambled in through the gate and down our concrete path. Gazing around, I realized nothing had changed. It was like walking through an old dream. I looked up at my bedroom above the front door. *That's where I'll be sleeping tonight.* Suddenly, I almost tripped over Mammy. I hadn't seen her crouched down weeding the small flower bed bordering the pathway. Her blue eyes widened in shock.

"Marcine?" she said a bit flustered.

My mouth wouldn't work.

She looked more anxious than I was. "Are you back now? For good?" In her voice were so many emotions—apprehension, hope, despair, happiness.

My breath caught as I suddenly realized how very much she'd missed me, had always loved me. That she'd never stopped worrying about me while I'd been gone. "Yes, I'm back." These three small words held so much meaning for both of us.

Walking towards her, I knew I was choosing to join the human world again, only this time I was ready for whatever challenge it might throw at me. My stray dogs had prepared me for any possible obstacle and the future no longer seemed frightening at all.

Mammy's big smile was a beautiful gift. I smiled back.

"Then it's vonderful to see you, Marcine. Come inside."